NORTHERNERS

NORTHERNERS

Profiles of People in the Northwest Territories

Douglas Holmes

James Lorimer & Company, Publishers
Toronto, 1989

Photo Credits: Northern News Services (Annie G. Robert; Richard Beck; René Fumoleau; Nick Sibbeston; Cece McCauley; Stephen Kakfwi; Lynda Sorensen; Peter Ittinuar; Nick Lebessis; John Todd; T. David Marshall; Edna Elias; Margaret Thrasher); Marina Devine (David Ruben Piqtoukun); Ministry of Culture and Communications, Government of the N.W.T. (Tagak Curley); Tusaayaksat (William Nasogaluak); Heather Cox (Doug Billingsley); Tessa Macintosh, Ministry of Culture and Communications, Government of the N.W.T. (Sharon Firth).

Canadian Cataloguing in Publication Data

Holmes, Douglas 1960-

Northerners

ISBN 1-55028-217-4 (bound) ISBN 1-55028-215-8 (pbk.)

1. Northwest Territories - Biographies. Northwest Territories - Description and travel - 1981- .* 3. Northwest Territories - Social life and customs.

I. Title.

FC4173.1.A1H65 1989 971.9'203'0922

F1060.92.H65 1989 C89-093554-8

James Lorimer & Company, Publishers
Egerton Ryerson Memorial Building
35 Britain Street
Toronto, Ontario M5A 1R7

Printed and bound in Canada
5 4 3 2 1 89 90 91 92 93

CONTENTS

For Mom and Dad

ACKNOWLEDGEMENTS

While talking politics over a cup of coffee at the Dene Cafe one day a few years ago, a woman suggested that I either run for MLA or write a book. Writing the book seemed to make the most sense. I thank her for the idea. I hope she knows who she is — I'm not sure if I do.

My life as a northern journalist may not have started while working for Jack Sigvaldason and Northern News Services, but it certainly took off then. A lot of the information in these pages was collected while working with Sig and his staff. I thank them for everything, including use of most of the photographs contained in this book.

Special thanks go to Judy Piercey and my sister, Nancy Holmes, for providing me with much needed advice and editorial help.

Many Northerners went out of their way to assist, and I extend my appreciation to: Raj Ahluwalia, Paul Andrew, Wayne Balinoff and the Indian Affairs staff in Yellowknife, Larry and Jennifer Bizanna, Ethel Blondin, Marc Bogan, the Bradley Air Service crew at Resolute Bay, Snookie Catholique, Shirley Connor, Stephen Conway, Doug Earl, William Firth, Jack Hicks, Gary Juniper, Kathryn King, Bernie Little, Tessa Macintosh, Margo McDiarmid, Shirley McGrath, Joanne McKenna, Dave McLaren, Isabel McNutt, Mary Nashook, Ootuk, Chris Rodgers, Elaine Schiman, Richard Spaulding, Fibbie Tatti and Bruce Valpy.

It would not have been possible to write the chapter about Annie G. Robert without material provided by the Gwitch'in Language Centre in Fort McPherson, and the chapter about Abe Okpik was enhanced by information contained in a document titled "Eskimo Identification and Disc Numbers" prepared for the Department of Indian Affairs and Northern Development by A. Barry Roberts.

Financial assistance was provided by the Northwest Territories Arts Council and the Ontario Arts Council.

I am grateful for the support and encouragement of Curtis Fahey and James Lorimer and Company Ltd.

I especially want to thank my mother, Rosalie Holmes, who introduced me to writing, and my father, Sandy Holmes, who introduced me to the North. To my parents, I dedicate this book.

Douglas Holmes
Yellowknife, N. W. T.

PREFACE

You could put every resident of the Northwest Territories into the Toronto Sky Dome and still have several thousand empty seats. But it is not likely that the 50,000 people who have scattered themselves across the 3.3 million square kilometers that make up the top third of Canada would all want to go to the Sky Dome.

The interests, activities, events and issues in which the people of the North are involved are different from any in southern Canada. And while the people are few in number, the human diversity in the northern territory is as great as anywhere else. There are the indigenous people — the Inuit of the Arctic barren lands and the Dene Indians of the Mackenzie River basin — who for generations have lived off the land hunting caribou or seal for their survival. There are Metis and white people who have adapted the traditional way of life, and others who have brought their own cultures to the North. All "Northerners," as committed residents of the Northwest Territories call themselves, are adapting to modern change, but at the same time they are fighting hard to remain unique. Dog teams may no longer be used on traplines, but they have become popular sporting events. Word processors and daisy-wheels are used in northern offices, but many spew out words in any of the Northwest Territories' seven aboriginal languages.

The ability of Northerners to change with the times on their own terms is dependent largely on the dismantling of the region's colonial political status. During the 1980s, as the Northwest Territories strives towards provincial status, the federal government has devolved powers ranging from health care to natural resources to the territorial government. And after years of rhetoric from politicians and native leaders, aboriginal land-claim "negotiations" are finally becoming land-claim "settlements." All northern politics during the 1980s have been dominated by one issue — the attempt to divide the Northwest Territories into two separate territories. The Inuit still have hopes to create "Nunavut," a sort of Inuit homeland in the eastern Arctic, even though discussions with the Dene and white people in the western Northwest Territories over where to draw a boundary line have been anything but straightforward.

I have had the fortunate opportunity to witness and become well acquainted with this remarkable decade in the North, since I first came to Yellowknife from Toronto for a visit (and ended up staying) in 1978, and especially since 1982 when I started my career as a journalist.

I have interviewed many Northerners over these years, and this book itself is based mostly on extensive interviews of the twenty-four individuals profiled and many others. The book does not pretend to be a comprehensive reference work about the Northwest Territories, but rather it gives a snapshot of the kind of people who make the North what it is today.

PART I
TRADITIONAL LIVES

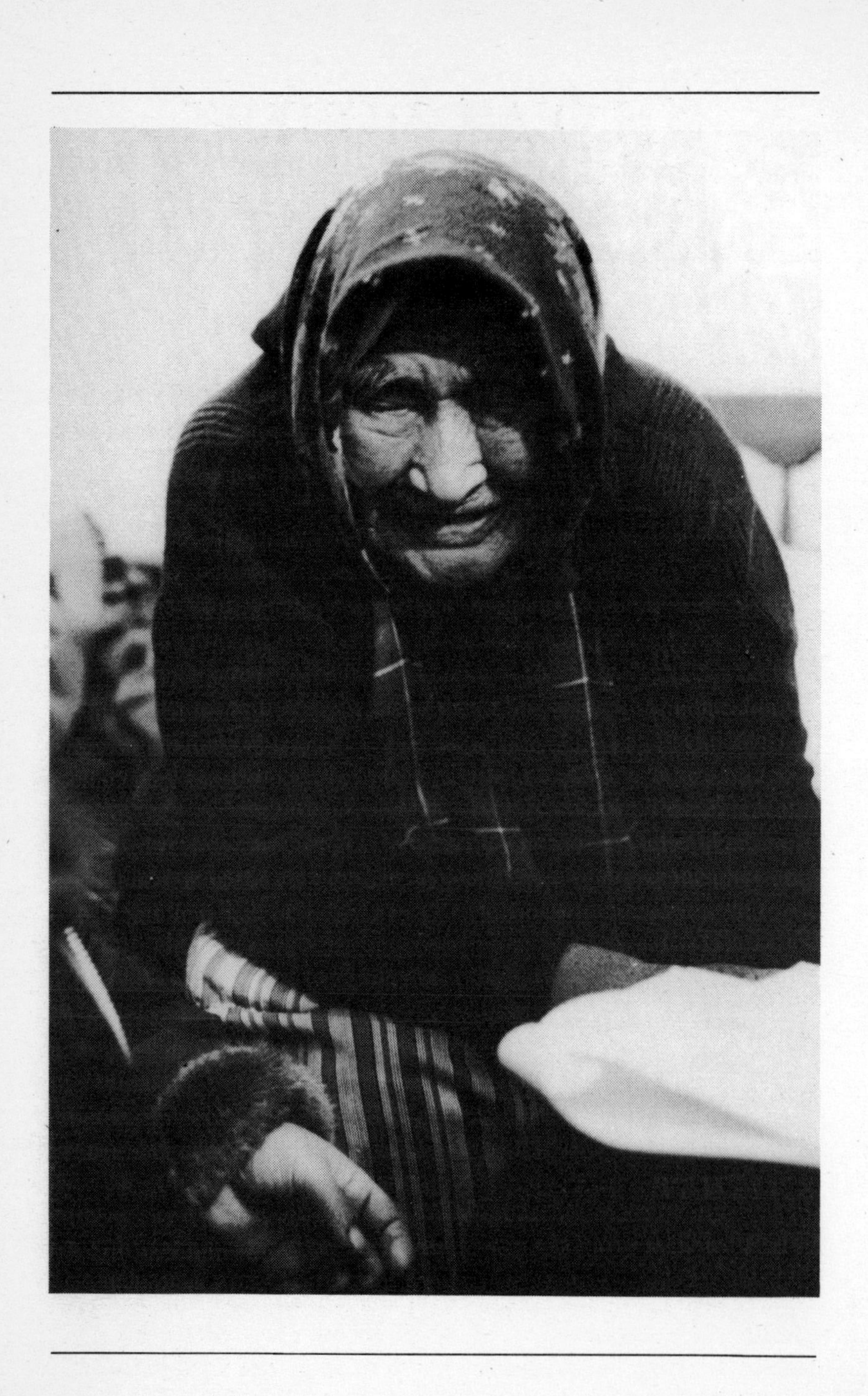

ANNIE G. ROBERT: ON THE LAND

Annie G. Robert was thirteen years old and alone in a bush camp with her two infant sisters. Her mother had just died and been buried by her father and brothers, who then left to continue their nomadic hunt for moose and caribou. Annie, suddenly the oldest female in the family, was left to pack up the tent and find her way to the next camp.

The year was 1893 — the Loucheaux Indians lived in tents year--round. Annie put her sisters in the sled; then she took down the tent and loaded the family belongings. She put a team of dogs in harness and set off down a narrow trail of snow through a dark forest of spruce and birch trees.

"I was crying all the time I was doing this," she recalled through a translation of her Loucheaux language, ninety years after that dreary winter day. "I kept looking back at my mother's grave, until I couldn't see it anymore. Then I really broke down and cried very hard."

She arrived at a site where other people were camped. She tried to set up her tent, but she did not know how. "So I cried again. A lot of good it did me; crying never helped."

Life for Annie Robert, and most other Loucheaux of her time, was little more than a continuous search for food and warmth. Both were scarce.

"I remember helping the dogs pull the sleds and they would fall from starvation. The dogs that froze would be left along the trail. Here and there you would see dead dogs. The people were starving too, but the dogs were all dead and the people had to pull the sleds."

She once watched an old man die of starvation. And a woman starved to death in her father's arms. "Those that did not have fresh meat were really poor. They only survived if someone gave them food.

"There were a lot of widows at that time. That's the way it was."

She recalled her brother shooting a moose after one famine. "My father was crying because he was happy that we had something to eat."

When one family had meat and another had none, the Loucheaux shared. Annie's family was once canoeing down the Peel River with a load of caribou. Other families were camped along the river bank and "they didn't have any meat. They found some bluefish and this is what they were living on. We landed and gave them fresh and dried meat. While we were there, some white people landed. They gave us some of the things they had. They gave me a bar of soap. They also gave us some useful things. We in turn gave them meat."

Annie was a young child when she first saw "white man's things." A group of Inuit brought tents, guns and pots and pans inland from the Arctic Ocean coast where there were white whalers. (To the Loucheaux, the Inuit were occasional enemies and occasional trading partners. This time, they came to trade.)

"A boy had what looked like a long skinny willow. It was a gun. First you would put a piece of rag in it, then the gun powder, the shell, another piece of rag, and then it was ready to go."

Their first gun was not very efficient, but it worked better than a bow and arrow. "Since the white man came, we have lived well. If there were no guns and shells, I don't know how it would be now."

The Loucheaux, one of the five Dene tribes, traditionally lived in the bush, following moose and migrating caribou around the area of what is today the northern portion of the Yukon-Northwest Territories border. At the turn of the century Fort McPherson was a nearby trading post where white people — Mounties, Hudson's Bay Company workers and missionaries — lived in a cluster of log cabins. The natives would come to Fort McPherson once every summer. They made a large boat out of 16 moose skins, loaded it with people and their belongings, including dogs, and paddled down the Peel River. They shot their way through rapids and, if the boat did not capsize, they would shout and fire their guns in the air to show their happiness. At Fort McPherson they took bales of dried caribou and moose meat to the Bay store. For one bale they received two cups of tea, two cups of flour and one cup of sugar. "We got very little for all that hard work, but no one complained," Annie said.

While in Fort McPherson in the summer of 1896, Annie's father re-married and then sixteen-year-old Annie married twenty-year-old Robert George. Annie had her first of twelve children three years later. That was when there were many rumours going around about the

Klondike gold rush. Annie and her husband decided to travel by dog team to a new boom town in the Yukon.

Dawson City was a cultural shock: 50,000 white people seeking their fortunes in gold, with hundreds more arriving everyday from the South. Hotels, taverns, casinos and dance halls were built overnight. Annie walked down the city's main street, with her baby packed on her back, admiring the strange wooden structures. In one building she noticed many people talking and laughing and dancing to loud music. She went to take a closer look, but her husband stopped her.

"Don't go in there. Don't even look."

They continued a little way past Dawson to where they had heard some Loucheaux were camped. When they arrived, they found thirty-seven people dead, likely from influenza brought in by the white man. "There were only a few orphans walking around. We saw them, but they also died one by one until there was no one left," Annie said.

After that horror, they started back to Fort McPherson. On the trail, in the middle of winter, Annie gave birth to another child. They stopped the dog team, delivered the baby, put it in the sled and carried on to the next camp site. "I thought for sure my child would freeze, but she lived."

Annie and Robert George eventually settled down at a semi-permanent camp at the foot of the Richardson Mountains, just inside the Yukon border. He trapped and hunted; she cleaned and skinned hides, cooked, sewed clothes, and raised her children as well as two grandchildren who were taken in after her son's wife died.

Robert George died in 1961. Annie stayed at the camp with her youngest son until 1974. She then moved to Fort McPherson, which by then had become the largest Loucheaux settlement in the region. She lived in a house and, in her later years, at the local senior citizen's home. But she continued to spend her summers on the land, at a fish camp on a nearby island in the Peel River where two daughters and two sons and their families lived.

In 1986, looking back on her 106 years of life, Annie had mixed feelings about the changes to her society brought about by the arrival of the white man. The introduction of alcohol was the worst thing to have happened, she said, and she was sorry that young people were losing the Loucheaux language.

She and most other elders could not speak English. With no means for the young to communicate, a painfully obvious generation gap prevailed. "I hear that the children are sent away to school. If they put them on the land, they wouldn't know what to do. They have learned the white man's way of life."

The arrival of the first priest was the best thing to have happened to the Loucheaux, she said. For a year or more after her mother's death, Annie's family stayed close to relatives, including an uncle who was an Anglican minister. After travelling all day, setting up her tent, and feeding the family, Annie would put her snowshoes back on in the evening and walk to a nearby tent for a church-like service.

Annie was also thankful that the white man's government gave her a warm bed and people brought her food. She received an old age pension, but, she said, "I feel that I'm stealing the money.

"We are kept warm by the oil the white people find. We have many white people working in our country; they work under ground, under sea and fly planes. I see all this and I am thankful and I pray to the Lord to look after them on their jobs. I also ask the Lord to give them what they are looking for."

Annie outlived seven of her twelve children. When she died in 1987, she was survived by fifty-seven grandchildren, 157 great-grandchildren, and sixty-one great-great-grandchildren. At least half of the 700 Loucheaux residents of Fort McPherson are related to Annie Robert, one way or another.

She kept track of the family tree at a time when surnames in the North were obscure or nonexistent. "We learned from her how important it was for us to be together as a family, to know who was our uncle and who were our cousins and who were our grandparents. She taught us everything," said Mary Teya, one of her granddaughters. "Boy, that woman knew what she was doing. That communication, the touching and the love that she showed us was really important. She would kiss everybody. I used to get really embarrassed when she would come over to me and hug me and kiss me. Now that's what I do with my grandchildren."

People went to Annie to draw upon her knowledge of Loucheaux history, language and culture. In her later years, she was frequently interviewed and her stories were recorded. "This machine with tape in it that I talk on is good for the younger generation," she said during a 1982 interview when she was 101. "We talk to people over the CBC radio station and I thank them for that."

After hearing her stories, people in Fort McPherson started to pay homage to their elders. Every November 27, Annie's birthday, a community feast and dance was held to honour all the old people. "One year, when Annie was 100 years old, she had a big cake," Teya said. "I don't know if there were 100 candles on it, but there were a lot anyway."

Annie enjoyed visitors, even strangers, coming to her room at the senior citizen's home, where all she did was "walk to the bathroom and walk around my bed." She told white guests that they were the first to talk to her since Prime Minister Pierre Trudeau. She met him in 1983 at the official opening of the Annie G. Robert Community Centre in Fort McPherson. "We talked for a long time about my life."

Local people would gather in her room and read from the Bible or sing hymns. "She couldn't see anymore, but she had that memory," Teya said. "She knew more of those hymns than we did, and we were reading them."

At her death on January 29, 1987, Annie was 106 years old — the oldest person in the Northwest Territories. Throughout her life she had been an example for her people. As much as anyone, she typified the strength of the Dene and their will to survive.

SUNLIGHT

ANNA NUNGAQ: RELOCATED TO TOTAL DARKNESS

For Anna Nungaq, it has been difficult enough just to live from one day to the next let alone perform her assigned role as an instrument of Canadian sovereignty in the Arctic.

She was paralyzed by polio at the age of two. Then in 1953, when she was twenty-seven, she and her parents were one of four Inuit families moved to Ellesmere Island from northern Quebec. They were part of a government plan to create a Canadian presence above the Northwest Passage by populating the previously uninhabited islands in the high Arctic.

Nungaq has wanted to "go back" to her home town of Port Harrison, now called Inukjuak, on the east coast of Hudson Bay, ever since she left. "We didn't want to come here. We didn't come here on our own. It was the government which sent us," she said at Grise Fiord, the most northerly community in Canada.

Speaking in Inuktitut, with a daughter interpreting, she continued: "A long time ago the Inuit used to say yes for anything. We believed the white people were very helpful. When they wanted us to move here, we said yes. We didn't know it was so far, so we just said yes to the government. Right now it's different because we don't just say yes to anything anymore."

When they left Quebec in September 1953, the four families packed all their possessions, including dogs and sleds, and boarded the supply ship, the C.D. Howe. When the Arctic sea was rough, which was most of the time, the passengers had to wear life jackets. Whenever they were not hanging on for their lives, doctors and nurses, dressed in white smocks with stethoscopes hanging around their necks, would examine them. The doctors found a child with hair lice and proceeded, without the consent of the parents, to give every boy and girl on board a brush cut. It was an Inuit belief at the time not to fight back when being abused. But they also believed that women were to have long hair, and some Inuit girls fought back. "My parents couldn't do anything about my being chased by a man with scissors," said Martha Flaherty, who was five years old when she was on the C.D. Howe. "I crawled under the bed. He actually crawled under to get me. I kicked him and kicked him. Then I locked myself and my mother in the washroom. We were both crying. It was like a bad dream. That person who chased me with the scissors will always be imprinted in my mind." (Flaherty got to keep her hair and even now, as an office worker in Ottawa, it falls below her waist.)

The families were shipped 2,000 kilometers north to a place called Craig Harbour, in southeast Ellesmere Island. It was as if they had landed on the moon. "They just dropped us off at a place where there were no buildings. It was dark and cold when we moved here and we had to stay in a tent," Nungaq recalled.

The families had been told they were going to a place where game was more plentiful. "The government told us a lie," said Nungaq.

There was in fact an abundance of wildlife in the area and, because of that, the settlement was considered a success. But the animals bore little resemblance to what Nungaq was accustomed to eating in Quebec. There were no ducks and geese, no eggs, no arctic char and shellfish, and very little caribou. Instead there were musk oxen and ringed seal. "It was very bad when we came here. We were hungry for our own food, for what we used to eat. What was here was no good."

The Quebec Inuit faced other hardships that neither they nor the Ottawa bureaucrats could have envisioned. They came from a region where rivers and lakes provided year-round drinking water. In the far north, fresh water was taken from the sea ice. It took years to develop the skill to recognize freshwater ice in the sea. Also, even though it was farther north, the sea around southern Ellesmere Island did not freeze as early as Hudson Bay because of currents and strong winds. The relocated hunters did not know the ice conditions and were not sure when it was safe to cross. As a result, they had to risk falling through the ice or miss much of the hunting season and go hungry.

They had no tea or bannock or other foods that they used to buy at the store in Inukjuak; there was no store on Ellesmere Island. The Mounties, the only white people in the area, sometimes had food, but to get any, the Inuit had to trade fur or animal skins. And the reason they had no food was the same reason they had no skins. So Inuit families would scrounge through the RCMP garbage and come home with empty tin cans and whatever leftovers the Mounties did not throw to their dogs.

Nungaq lived in tents, sod houses, or igloos in the winter, for her first eleven years on Ellesmere Island. There was very little contact with the outside world — no airplanes or boats ever came by — and she heard nothing about the relatives she had left behind in Quebec.

The relocated Quebecers shared their settlement with a group of Inuit who had been relocated from the Pond Inlet area of northern Baffin Island. The Baffin Inuit were supposed to help the Quebec Inuit adjust to the high Arctic. The government planners did not realize that tribal rivalries and different language dialects might lead to hostility between the two groups. By 1958, after the size of both groups had grown through births and further migration, the Quebec Inuit moved a couple of miles away and set up a separate camp.

By 1964, the federal government built a school and some houses a few miles east, at the present-day location of Grise Fiord. The two Inuit camps moved in to consolidate the new settlement, but today they still live at opposite ends of town, and they rarely marry someone from the other side.

To Nungaq, the establishment of Grise Fiord meant she could move out of her tent and into a small shack built from scrap lumber. She was finally given a house in 1967, fourteen years after she left Quebec.

Nungaq was married in Grise Fiord, to a man who was also relocated from Quebec. He died in the fall of 1987 after falling through the ice while polar bear hunting.

Nungaq moved around in a specially-built sled in the winter and a wheelchair in the summer, but she was losing the strength of her arms in her old age. She spent most of her time in recent years sitting on a foam mattress on her living room floor — within reach of her television remote control, radio, telephone and two-way radio to keep contact with hunting camps. She said that she wanted the support of her family in Quebec, including two brothers and an uncle.

"It has been so long since I have seen my relatives. Most of my relatives are old and they are dying. I want to move back to see them while we are all still alive."

In the summer of 1988, at the age of sixty-two, Anna Nungaq returned to Inukjuak.

After several years of negotiations with Makivik Corporation, the organization that represents the Inuit of northern Quebec, the federal government agreed in 1987 to pay the moving expenses and build houses in Inukjuak for those relocated people and their families who wanted to return. The agreement also included an admission, for the first time, from the government that the true intent of the relocation was to establish Canadian sovereignty in the Arctic.

Nungaq raised all five of her children in Grise Fiord. To them, Grise Fiord is home. Whether to stay or to go to Inukjuak with their mother was a difficult decision. In the end, two would stay, two would go, and one would leave Grise Fiord, but to go to Calgary rather than Quebec.

Daughter Alicee Nowra did not think that her mother would suffer if she and her siblings did not accompany her to Quebec; the relatives in Quebec could look after her as well or better than her children in Grise Fiord, who were working and raising their own families. But Nowra said it was important for her to be near her mother. She was still learning traditional Inuit skills such as sewing and scraping skins from her mother. Anna Nungaq also helped raise Nowra's four children, especially since her own husband died in a hunting accident in 1984. So Nowra also moved to Inukjuak, but she did not know for how long. "I think I might end up coming back (to Grise Fiord) because I really don't know about Quebec. I don't know where to go hunting, I don't know if I'll be working."

Nowra had lived with her grandmother in northern Quebec for a few years as a teenager. At that time, she had found it difficult to get used to the regular amounts of sunlight. To the people of Grise Fiord, which is located 1,100 kilometers inside the Arctic Circle, total darkness in the winter and total daylight in the summer are normal. "And I missed the mountains," she said. "It's flat there (in northern Quebec) and it's always windy." Grise Fiord, which is surrounded by mountains in three directions and the Northwest Passage to the south, is often rated the most beautiful community in the North. But when the Inuit were first relocated to the area, the young ones were intimidated by the "mean-looking" mountains and thought they might come crushing down on top of them.

Aside from the geography, Nowra also did not trust Inukjuak's demographics. Its population of 700 may mean it is "too big" a place to raise her children. "There are so many people there, they might get into something bad, like taking drugs. I want them to get good schooling because I didn't finish school and I didn't get a good job. I don't want them to be like me."

Inukjuak has a reputation for high drop-out rates and illicit drugs in the schools. Grise Fiord, on the other hand, is one of the rare northern communities that does not have a noticeable problem with alcohol or drug abuse. Friends teased Nowra's younger sister, Martha Nungaq, that if she moved to Inukjuak she would become a drug addict. They also raised fears that she would not be able to understand anyone in Quebec. After the years of isolation and sharing the community with the Baffin Inuit, the Inuktitut language in Grise Fiord had a dialect that was different from Inukjuak's.

Although Anna Nungaq tried, she could not persuade Martha and her youngest daughter, Lydia, to leave Grise Fiord. Lydia, who was twenty-two years old when her mother left, said she had a good job working as the interpreter at the Grise Fiord nursing station and "I don't think there are any openings in Quebec."

It will feel strange living in her home community without her mother and sister, Lydia Nungaq said, but "I'll have to get used to it." After they move to Quebec, "I think they'll want to come back here. They're used to this place." Whether to move back or not was the hot topic of conversation and debate in Grise Fiord in 1987 and 1988. Most people shared Lydia's thoughts. They thought the people who were moving back to Quebec "don't know how good they have it here." They could not see the benefits of moving from a community that is served by a northern territorial government that is sensitive to the aboriginal people, to a community served by a southern-based provincial government that pays little attention to its northland or its native peoples. Inuit children in Northwest Territories schools learn Inuktitut, while in Quebec, "maybe they'll have to learn French," said Alicee Nowra.

Those opposed to the move saw Inukjuak as a place of high unemployment, whereas almost everybody in Grise Fiord who wants a wage-paying job, has one. A couple of people drive the water delivery truck, a couple of people run the co-op store, a couple more run the hotel. There is the town manager, and many are full time hunters. Since there were only about 100 residents of Grise Fiord, about half of whom were children, it did not take many jobs to provide full employment. The Grise Fiord residents who decided to move to Inukjuak tended to be those on the lower end of the local income scale. Nowra worked part time as a janitor at the Grise Fiord hamlet office. Anna Nungaq did not have a job; she lived on her monthly $296 welfare and pension cheque.

Nungaq did not return to Quebec earlier because she was waiting for permission from the government. The government sent her there and, after all the years, she still held the notion that the government would have to send her back. "Since we came here on what seems like a free trip, we want them to move us back."

Nungaq is not angry at anyone, not even the government, because it took her so long to go back. On the contrary, she was delighted that she was able to return at all. So, almost as she had done in 1953, Nungaq and nineteen others loaded all their belongings, including snowmobiles (which by then had replaced dogs) and sleds, onto a chartered Twin Otter aircraft. They were airlifted out of Grise Fiord on July 19, 1988. They transferred onto a jet at Resolute Bay and twenty-four hours later, or thirty-five years later to Anna Nungaq, they arrived at Inukjuak: Home.

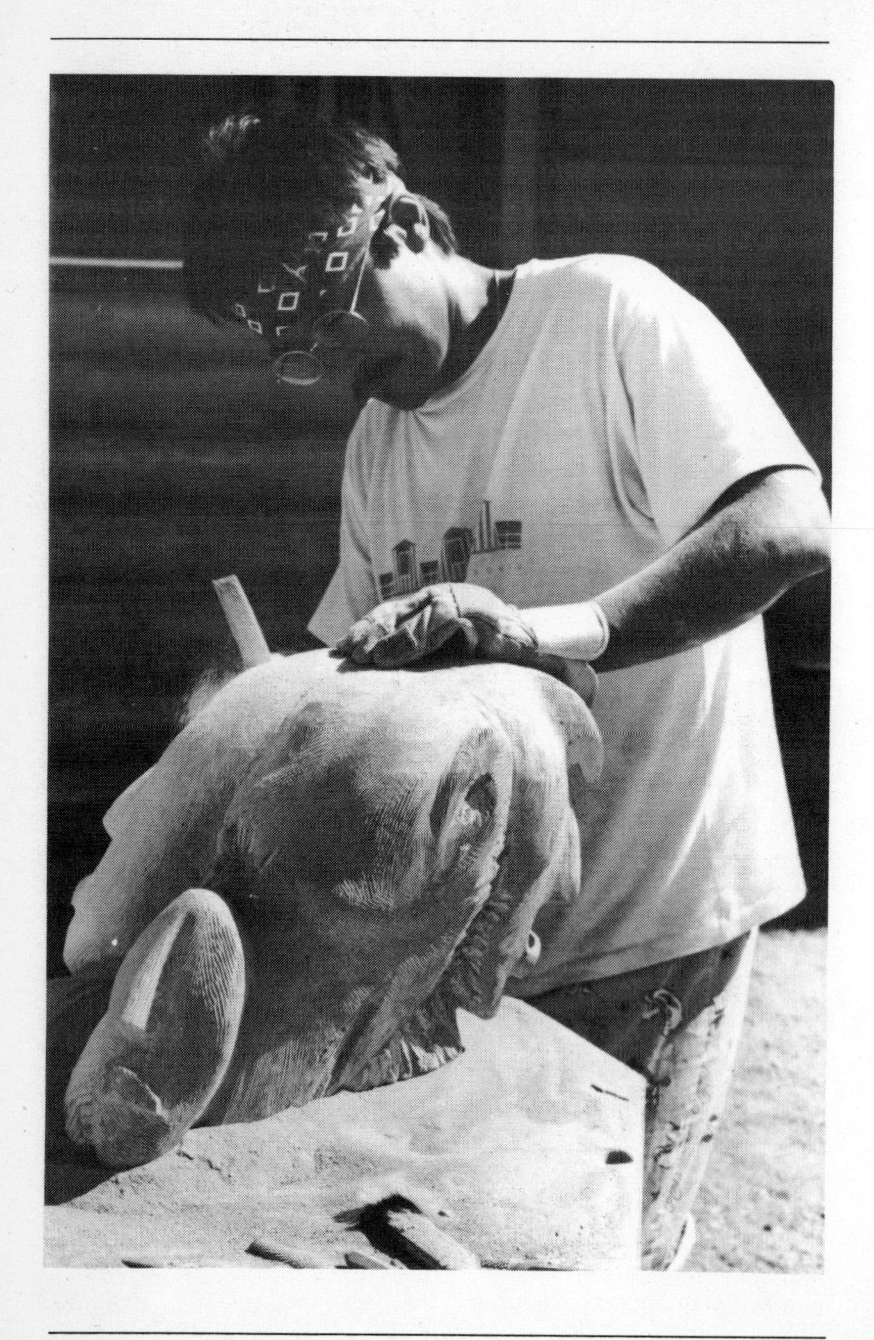

DAVID RUBEN PIQTOUKUN: POLAR BEARS IN AFRICA

Today, some of the most traditional northern sculpture is carved out of Brazilian soapstone by an Inuk who lives in Toronto and who uses power tools.

David Ruben Piqtoukun has emerged in the 1980s as one of the "new generation" of Inuit artists who are reviving old legends and myths through their work. Piqtoukun's sculptures are abstract images of shamans and demons, as Inuit art was before sculptors started selling their work to Southerners who wanted a polar bear carving that looked like a polar bear.

Piqtoukun is a self-taught artist. His ideas come from listening to the old Inuvialuit legend-tellers in his home town of Paulatuk, on the Arctic Ocean coast, where he returns to visit once a year to "get the city out of my system." Further ideas come from the stories that frightened him as a child and that still come back to haunt him in his dreams.

Some of his finished sculptures even scare him, especially one called "Allioks," which means "to be afraid" in his native language. The soapstone carving is based on a story of a young couple who were travelling on the land in the winter. The wife gave birth to twins, but she was too sick to care for them and they died. The couple buried the children in the snow and continued travelling. Demonic spirits then entered the twins' souls and bodies, and they grew up with enormous heads and mouths. They found their parents and crushed them with their sharp teeth.

"To incorporate that story," Piqtoukun said, "I carved a very large, spooky-looking face with enlarged eyes and teeth from ear to ear using caribou and polar bear teeth, which are real rugged." The sculpture, completed in 1985, is part of the McMichael Canadian art collection at Kleinburg, Ontario. It is too powerful and scary for a private collection, he said. "It belongs in a museum."

After carving such pieces, Piqtoukun finds it difficult not to believe in Shamanism. Before the introduction of Christianity, the Inuit believed in shamans who could transform themselves into animals. The local shaman was not only the Inuit's spiritual leader and healer but also the artist who carved masks for ceremonial purposes. "In this day and age, the artist could be an extension of the shaman," Piqtoukun suggested. "Certain objects that I create draw so much power, you're tapping into something that maybe you're not too familiar with. It's a gift. It's an interesting gift."

One of Piqtoukun's favourite images is the polar bear, from which he draws "a lot of strength and energy." Several of his works are bear/man images — a bear with a man's face protruding from its hip or paws. Or he emphasizes and elongates various parts of the bear — its teeth, its shoulders, or especially its neck to show the animal's movement. His "self-portrait" and the work he regards as his "most significant" is a large angry polar bear that he carved in 1984. By then he had been living in Toronto for three years but was still finding it difficult to adapt to the city. "You can feel a lot of tension in that piece. It's how I felt inside of me at the time. After I produced it, I travelled up to the Arctic to get myself back together."

When he returns each year to visit Paulatuk, Piqtoukun spends many days hunting and fishing on the tundra and sleeps in a tent at night to take in the fresh Arctic air. In the community, he sits and listens patiently to the old timers who tell the stories that will later become the subject of his carvings. In Paulatuk, his idea bank is replenished. "When somebody talks, I think sculpture."

And while a rock looks like a rock to most people, Piqtoukun sees in a stone something that is almost alive. "Soapstone comes in odd shapes, so I study the shapes for a long time and at some point I can see an image. I can see some protrusion that resembles an arm or a face and take it from there."

He works mostly with Brazilian soapstone because of its good quality and because soapstone quarries in the North are becoming depleted. He has also used jade, marble, granite, Italian crystal, alabaster, African wonderstone and Arizona pipestone. Piles of whalebone, caribou antlers and ivory from the North, which are used to decorate the stone sculptures, clutter his Toronto garage-turned-studio. A wide variety of materials is accessible in Toronto, and the city offers a large market. Most Inuit artists in the North take their finished carvings to the local co-op and accept whatever money they are offered.

Piqtoukun markets his own artwork and has become so sought-after that his carvings sell for between $2,500 and $8,000.

Most of his work has been sold to wealthy private collectors. His rare public showings have received much praise from all sorts of people.

Jean Blodgett, the adjunct curator of Inuit art at the Art Gallery of Ontario, considers Piqtoukun "a major figure in the contemporary field." Prince Andrew, stopping in to see a Piqtoukun exhibit in Yellowknife while enroute to a canoe trip on the barrenlands in 1987, remarked: "I have seldom seen such strength and tradition brought out in Inuit carvings as in this work."

Some critics have said that Piqtoukun is not an authentic Inuit artist because he lives in Toronto and carves Brazilian soapstone. But there is no resentment in Paulatuk, where he is regarded as an ambassador teaching southern people about the Arctic. Piqtoukun's wife, Esther, defends her husband further: "Nobody criticized Picasso because he lived in France instead of Spain."

Esther is another reason Piqtoukun lives in Toronto. She is a born-and-raised Torontonian whom he met at an art gallery. They live in an old brick house in a quiet part of the city with their Siberian husky, Sikoo. The dog and the varied collection of native art that fills the home are constant reminders of his roots.

Yet Piqtoukun has not lived a traditional Inuit lifestyle since he was taken away from his nomadic parents and placed in a residential school before he was five years old. He dropped out when he was seventeen years old and tried without success to be a hunter. (By 1988, at the age of thirty-eight, he still had not killed a polar bear, the traditional Inuit test of manhood.) In 1968, when he was eighteen, he went to Edmonton, "where I was lost." He took various labour jobs in Alberta, including work on oil rigs, but always quit or was fired after a couple months. He met his brother, Abraham, in Calgary in 1972 and they hitch-hiked to the west coast. In Vancouver, Abraham, who had studied art at the University of Alaska, introduced carving to his brother. (Abraham still lives in British Columbia and has become a successful artist himself, specializing in bronze castings.) At first, David Piqtoukun carved pendants depicting Arctic animals and sold them to a gallery at the entrance of Stanley Park. "I had to find some sort of income and I realized I could do it through stone carving. That's how it all started."

He progressed from pendants to jade. Carving jade taught him patience and discipline, as well as how to use high-speed power tools. "You can't just carve or chisel jade. You have to grind it into shape. I was used to creating things that were instant. You have an idea, you go out and carve it. But with jade, you really have to go through the whole long process." It took a full year to carve a jade falcon in flight. It had a seventeen-inch wing span with flared tips that were almost paper thin. He was relieved to finish it without breaking any of the points.

After ten years in Vancouver, Piqtoukun was "exhausted" and suffering from "sculptor's block" — a rock was starting to look like a rock again. He packed his carving tools and drove across the country. He reached Toronto, about 6,500 kilometers southeast of Paulatuk, and started carving his way back to the mythology of his boyhood. In Vancouver, he carved for money. In Toronto, after collecting the old Inuvialuit stories, he carved to regain his lost culture. "At some point you mature along with your work and you go that extra distance. Once you've hit your quality peak as an artist, you can't go any lower."

At an artists' workshop in Iqaluit, on Baffin Island, in February 1988, Piqtoukun encouraged other Inuit artists, many of whom carve simply to supplement their regular hunting and trapping incomes, to be professional about their work. He told them to take pride in their art — do not carve what the Co-op store or the white man wanted them to carve, but carve what was in their imagination. He also introduced them to a local granite that could be carved when soapstone was scarce. And he taught them how to work with the harder rock — by using electric chisels and grinders and drills and sand blasters.

This was all new to the artists of Baffin Island. Furthermore, they knew very little about David Ruben Piqtoukun. They had never seen his work; he had had only two exhibits in the North, both at the other end of the vast territory, in Yellowknife and Inuvik. But when they were shown photographs of his carvings, they were amazed at the creativity and the quantity. The Baffin artists took to the new carving techniques so readily that, before long, dust caused by the power tools filled the air in the workshop room and everyone needed breathing masks, safety glasses and ear plugs. Then the fuses blew.

Piqtoukun also has given demonstrations at the Northwest Territories pavilion at Expo '86 in Vancouver, and in 1982 the federal government invited him to participate in a week-long Canadian trade and culture fair in the Ivory Coast. During his first day in Abidjan, the country's capital city, he took his tools to a television station where a three-hour special on Canada was being taped. During the filming, the cameras occasionally would turn to Piqtoukun as he blasted away on a carving of a polar bear cub, filling the studio with dust. In the following days, at demonstration booths on the trade show site and in a hotel lobby, he completed what had to be the first polar bear carved out of African wonderstone. He produced two more carvings that week, and got into a rhythm of working and talking at the same time, as the local people asked him many questions about his work and the Arctic. A French interpreter (the Ivory Coast was formerly a colony of France) accompanied Piqtoukun, except at the event's closing banquet. There, after several long speeches in French, which Piqtoukun did not understand, the Inuit artist was asked to stand up. When he did, to his surprise, there was great applause.

The only time he really felt out of place in the Ivory Coast was during his demonstrations in the hotel lobby. There he carved in front of a stuffed polar bear and a styrofoam replica of an igloo. "It's amazing some of the silliness you have to put up with, but then again, who there had ever seen an igloo before? I just shrugged and continued to work."

(Life for an Inuk in southern Ontario can be equally absurd. A cement-blocks association once asked Piqtoukun to pose for a trade magazine advertisement. He put on a parka and mukluks when it was eighty-five degrees outside, stood on thirty pounds of sugar in the middle of the football stadium, and built an igloo out of cement blocks while keeping a smug look on his face.)

In the Ivory Coast, Piqtoukun found remarkable similarities between the Inuit and African ceremonial masks. In 1986, as his contribution to a travelling exhibition organized to raise money for African famine relief, he incorporated elements of both the Inuit and African cultural traditions into a painting of a mask. "This painting is a statement of my hope that the combined powers of Sedna, the Inuit Sea Goddess, and the Ivory Coast Harvest Mask will bring food and prosperity to the people of the Ivory Coast," he wrote at the time.

In 1988, the United Nations set up a trust fund from the sale of prints from another painting on which Piqtoukun and a Dene artist, Dolphus Cadieux, had collaborated. The fund will permit northern artists to work outside the country, and foreign artists to come to the Northwest Territories. "I think it's important that your work eventually takes you abroad. It broadens your minds a little bit, and that affects the quality of your work," Piqtoukun said.

Inuit art is becoming increasingly popular outside Canada, especially in the United States, where Canadians who retire or relocate are spreading the word. Piqtoukun's works have been shown at a museum in Arizona, and Ottawa has asked him to create a major installation at the entrance to their new embassy in Washington, D.C. The display will include a seven-foot high inukshuk, a traditional Inuit landmarker made of rock that usually is in the shape of a human.

Piqtoukun built a similar inukshuk in 1988, in the lobby of a new government building in Edmonton. To have created such a culturally significant work in the Alberta capital was symbolic. He had arrived in Edmonton exactly twenty years earlier as a lost child from the North.

SPONSORED
By
Back Bay Welding
YELLOWKNIFE N.W.T.

RICHARD BECK: DOG MUSHING DYNASTY

One of the North's greatest leaders answers to the name of "Friendly."

She is strong, keen, energetic and, of course, friendly. In appreciation for a job well done, people often pat her on the back, and on the head, and even scratch her behind the ears. Friendly is a dog — the lead dog for champion musher Richard Beck.

Friendly and a team of nine other canines have footed some big wins for Beck on the sled dog racing circuit, including four Canadian and two World titles.

The Canadian Championship Dog Derby is held on Beck's home turf in Yellowknife each March, at the end of the dog-racing season. Although many people thought it was a "fluke" when he first won it in 1983, "King Richard" has since become a local sports hero. He received unprecedented recognition in 1988, when he won five of the last six races of the fourteen-race season, including the Canadian championship, which he won for the third time in a row.

Richard Beck is the latest in the Beck dynasty of dog mushers. In 1957, Uncle Ray won a race in his home community of Rocher River, then drove his six dogs 100 miles in two days across Great Slave Lake, and arrived in time to win the Yellowknife derby. Uncle Ray won the Yellowknife race three times, and another uncle won it a record five times. A cousin and his older brother, Grant, have also been Canadian champions. In the 1988 race, Richard faced his brother, two cousins and his sixteen-year-old son, John.

What is it like competing against all those relatives?

"They're just another team that you have to pass."

Even your own son?

"Well, I coach him along, but I make sure he gets my worse dogs so he doesn't beat me," he said with a chuckle. "If he's coming on too strong I tell him to slow down or else he's grounded for a month."

The family's pre-eminent mushing status seems solid for another generation. John finished second to his father in the 1988 Canadian championship, using Richard's spare dogs. And daughter Heather was just sixteen months old when she entered her first children's race. She was strapped onto the sled with scarfs and belts, and she won.

The racing Becks come from a large Metis family of trappers who used dogs to work on traplines spread across the south shore of Great Slave Lake. Richard had two dogs of his own in the 1950s, while growing up in the settlement of Fort Resolution. There was no trucked or running water at that time, so Beck provided a door-to-door delivery service, using his dogs to pull along a forty-five-gallon barrel. When he was 14 years old, he and his immediate family moved to Yellowknife, but his dogs were left behind.

It was about ten years later, when Beck was reading water meters for the City of Yellowknife, that he came across a house with a litter of pups in the back yard. The owner said that he could take them, but Beck decided he did not want dogs. That weekend he watched a local dog race and brother Grant won it easily. Too easily, thought Richard. Sibling rivalry prompted him to go back and get the pups. He brought them home and told his wife that he was going to become a dog musher.

"I thought it was the stupidest thing that I had ever heard of," Vi Beck recalled. "I was really pissed off. I didn't want dog shit all over the carpet."

But she soon "started to pretend" that she liked the animals and helped her husband organize his races and collect sponsorship money. Now, she said, "we can't quit."

Richard and Vi Beck have been together since they were both teenagers. They went through a troubled period where all they seemed to do was get drunk and fight. Their relationship improved after they got the dogs, "perhaps because it gave us something to concentrate on," Vi said. "We learned responsibility. We learned to work with animals."

The dogs are only raced during the winter, but they have to be cared for, exercised and fed year-round. They eat ground chicken, ground pork, liver, eggs, wheat germ oil, and "a little bit of dog food, but not too much," Richard said.

Vi mused that "they eat better than we do." (At least one cleaning woman would disagree. While on the racing circuit, Richard often thaws out mounds of chicken and liver in the hotel room bathtub. One time a maid thought she saw a dead body in the tub and ran screaming out of the bathroom. "Oh," said the musher. "It must be the dogs' food.")

Beck's dogs are not the average household pets. Each one costs about $1,500, and in Europe, where the sport's popularity is rapidly increasing with an annual 660-mile race through the Alps, they have been sold for $10,000. The dogs, called "Alaskans," are specially bred for racing. They are part hound, for speed, and part Siberian husky, for endurance. Their instinct is to run. "As soon as you take them out of the truck when you get to a race, their back legs start shaking," Beck said. "And it's not because they're cold."

Sometime the dogs are too eager. Once, the dog running point (behind the lead) tripped over the paws of Beck's lead dog and then all the other dogs became tangled together. The other teams raced past as the point, pinned by the other dogs, lay flat on his back. They soon straightened out and were about to pass another team when the handles on the sled snapped. Beck fell off and the dogs kept going. He had to run through deep snow for about a mile to catch up to them, and then finished the last thirty miles of the fifty-mile race crouched on the handle-less sled. Beck still managed to finish sixth.

The Alaskans can move at over twenty miles an hour. They can urinate without breaking stride and some breeders claim they can even run and sleep at the same time. Vi thought she may have caught one napping. "I don't know if he was asleep, but that dog's eyes were definitely closed. I couldn't believe it."

The multi-talented racers are nothing like Uncle Ray's big working dogs that would stop and relax while he set his traps. Until the early 1980s, teams of working dogs would come fresh off the trapline and compete against the streamlined Alaskans in the Yellowknife derby. But then dog mushing became a more professional sport and the slower trapline dogs were eventually excluded from the competition. They made the race look like it belonged in the "bush league" and organizers sought to create an image of the three-day, 150-mile Canadian championship as one of the most prestigious stops on the North American racing circuit. The prize money is boosted almost every year. In 1988, it was $30,000, with $9,000 going to the winner. By the mid 1990s, the purse is expected to reach $100,000.

As for the trapline dogs, they have disappeared completely from many northern settlements and their howls have been replaced with the roar of snowmobile engines. According to Beck, "if it wasn't for racing, there'd hardly be any dogs around. The sport is holding up the northern tradition of dog teams, no doubt about it."

Sled dog racing has adopted many of the cultural and traditional aspects of its trapping roots. The seventeen-pound, custom-built racing sled is similar in design to the sled used for generations by natives in Alaska and the Yukon. And many mushers wear trapline clothing such as mukluks while racing. They almost all wear fur hats and the competition for the most ingenious hat can be as fierce as the contest on the trail.

A sled dog race is usually the premiere attraction of a local spring carnival, a traditional event recalling the days when trappers came out of the bush after a long winter to celebrate Easter with games and feasts. The Canadian Championship Dog Derby, shorter dog races, children's races, and a competition to see which dog can pull the most weight are held over the three days of Yellowknife's Caribou Carnival. It also features snowshoe races, muskrat skinning and tea boiling contests, and other events based on bush skills.

Richard and Vi Beck travel with twenty-two dogs on a circuit of the northern territories, western provinces and northwestern states. They drive during the week and race on the weekend. "I'm a full-time truck driver and a part-time dog musher," said Richard, who shares the driving with Vi.

While Richard is racing, Vi videotapes the start, finish and as much of the middle of each race as possible. Richard watches them between heats and "studies them just like they do in hockey." He can gauge which of his dogs are tiring, something that is not so easy to do during the race when he is looking at their rear ends.

Mushers cannot replace dogs from one heat to another, but they are allowed to drop as many as they wish. The size of dog teams usually are reduced each race day, since a tired dog slows down the others. During a race, Beck thinks about how hard he should be pushing his dogs. He does not want to exhaust them early in case their energy is needed for a close finish.

Races vary in length, from ten-mile sprints to three-day marathons of 150 miles. Beck prefers the long-distance runs because they require greater strategy. "Anyone can do a sprint race. You just run flat out all the way around for twenty miles."

While racing, Beck wears a portable headset under his fur hat to listen to live radio broadcasts and find out if other mushers are coming on strong. Whips are not allowed during a race, so if the dogs have to shift gear, mushers yell out a command such as "haw" or "yah" or some other sound which means nothing to human ears. What you say is not important; it is how you say it. Dogs respond not to words, but to tones of the voice. And contrary to popular belief, mushers do not say "mush."

"Mush is porridge," Beck said.

A musher usually rides along on the sled that the dogs pull — he does the thinking while they do the work. But sometimes he helps the team go faster by pushing with a foot. In winning the 1987 Canadian championship, Beck had to push for the last twenty miles.

Dog racing is a sport where male and female — people and dogs — compete as equals. Beck's dog team is a mixture of both. And like any sport, the energetic but inexperienced rookies are balanced with the slower but wiser veterans. Choosing which dog to use on any particular race day can also depend on weather and snow conditions. Some dogs are trained to run through deep snow, others are best on hard ice. Or some may be long-distance runners while others are sprinters. But Beck is beating the odds in all respects by training his dogs somewhere in the middle. They are known for their marathon victories, but they win sprints as well.

Beck starts training his dogs in late August by having them run in front of his pick-up truck, "even though it's hard on the transmission." They start pulling a sled when there is enough snow on the ground. He and his son each take out one team a day, starting with jaunts of two or three miles and gradually increasing to thirty-five miles. They run only fifty miles in a race.

Beck has forty dogs, which is a small kennel by racing standards. It was considered an incredible feat in racing circles when Beck's two teams — half his kennel — placed first and second in the 1988 Canadian championship. Most mushers own more than fifty dogs and they sometimes pool dogs from various kennels to form a sort of canine all-star team. But Beck is careful about lending out his dogs. A musher from Minnesota once offered $6,000 to use his team for one race. Beck could have just watched the race and counted the money, but he turned him down because "if one dog got hurt, it wouldn't have been worth it."

It costs Beck about $20,000 a year to feed and keep his dogs. With his race earnings, he broke even in 1987 and made money for the first time in 1988. It helps to have the sponsorship of a Yellowknife welding company, which gives him a credit card to pay for his gas to drive from one circuit race to another. "We may be broke and starving, but at least we'll always get home," Vi said.

Richard Beck has not given up his day job with the city works department, and he uses his regular vacation days to compete on the circuit. He trains the dogs after work, in the dark, and he usually does not get home until after one o'clock in the morning. Beck would like to mush his way to the point where he can take a summer job and devote the entire winter to the dogs. There are such professional dog mushers in Alaska, where sled dog racing is the state sport, where children know the names of all the top mushers and their lead dogs, and where corporations contribute large amounts of sponsorship dollars.

Once he becomes a full-time dog musher, Richard Beck will know that both he and his sport have arrived in Canada.

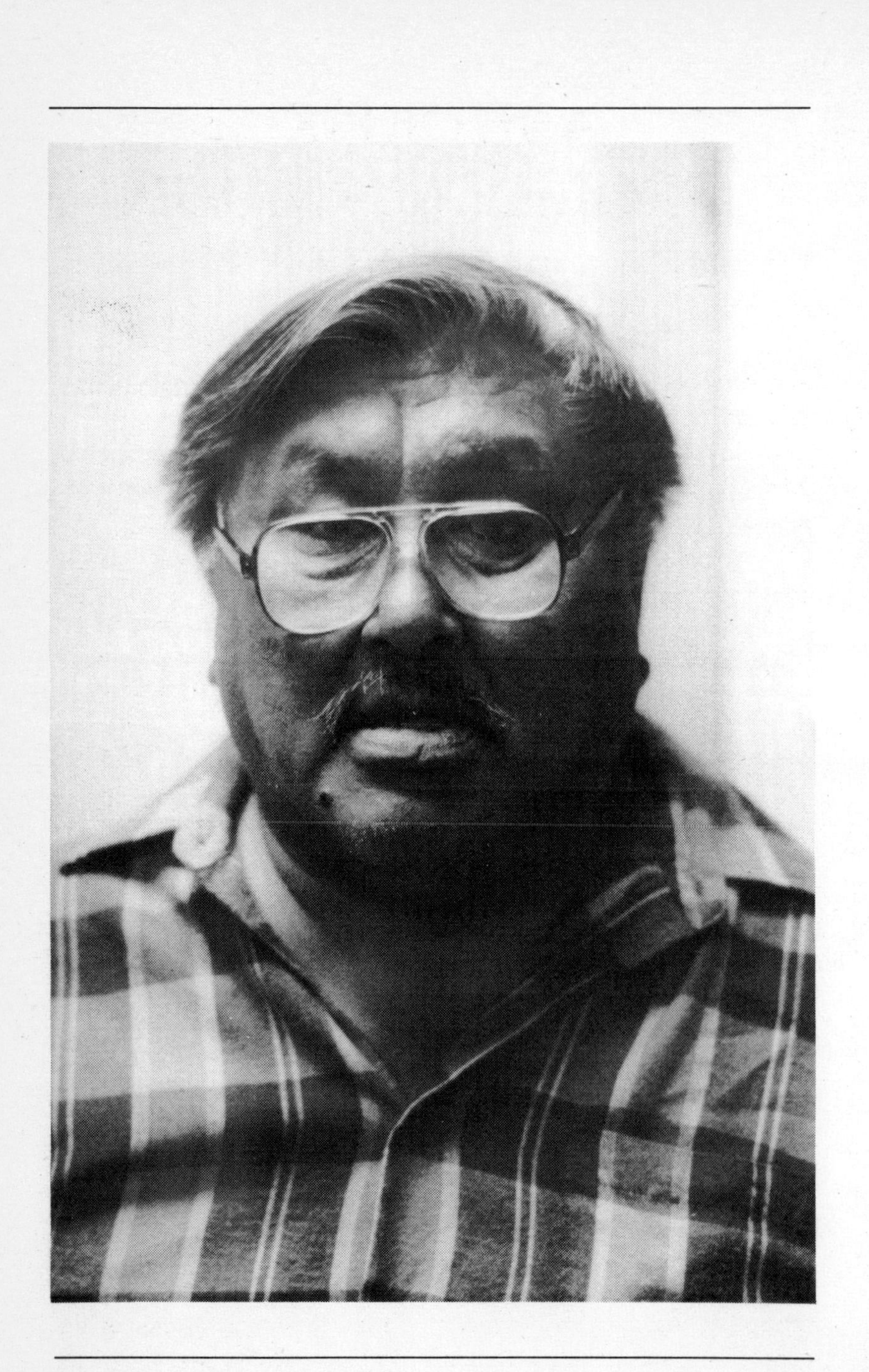

ABE OKPIK: PROJECT SURNAME

Abe Okpik wore a dog tag. It was stamped with his serial number, W3-554. He was never in the army, but he is an Inuk.

Until 1971, all Canadian Inuit were issued, at birth, an identification number stamped on a thin fibre disc about the size of a quarter with two small holes punched in it so it could be worn around the neck or wrist. It was the government's way of keeping track of the Inuit. Using their names was too complicated. Family allowance, old age pension and pay cheques were issued to numbers rather than names. No Inuk had a social insurance number. The all-purpose disc number served just fine.

But times were changing and after enough people started to think it was anachronistic to make native people carry numbers, the federally appointed commissioner of the Northwest Territories, Stu Hodgson, launched "Project Surname."

Abe Okpik was hired to replace the numbers with names. He was the best, and perhaps only, person for the job. He was a jovial type. He always had a good story or joke to tell, and he was popular across the Arctic. He was a native, but also a career civil servant, which pleased Ottawa. Okpik learned the countless dialects of Inuktitut on his own in Ottawa while working for the government in the early 1960s. The job, Okpik said, included "answering letters and inquiries from people who were wondering about their relatives who had gone to hospitals down south. The government needed somebody who could respond to them in their language." (Okpik spent several years in southern hospitals himself. First he hurt his leg on a trapline on the Mackenzie River Delta, where he grew up. He still walks with a limp. Later he was treated for tuberculosis.) From Ottawa, Okpik transferred to Frobisher Bay (now called Iqaluit) on Baffin Island. He worked in a rehabilitation centre for hospital patients returning from the South. "Some of the people were so weak they couldn't recuperate on the land because it was so rough and tough and cold. You couldn't just take them from a hospital bed and throw then into a camp."

He moved to Yellowknife in 1965 where he helped a group of Inuit hard rock miners and their families adjust to the white urban culture. The Inuit had been sent to work in the local gold mines after a nickel mine in Rankin Inlet shut down. While in Yellowknife, Okpik became the first native appointed to the territorial council, the forerunner to the legislative assembly. Most of the councillors were then appointed by the government, rather than elected by the people. Many were Ottawa bureaucrats who "knew this country real well without ever walking on it," Okpik said. They met in Ottawa for a few weeks a couple of times each year. During Okpik's two years on the council, they met in the Northwest Territories just once, in Resolute Bay in 1967. The commissioner ran the show. He drew his power from laws written in 1867, when his job was to keep law and order in the Old West. He had the power to order taverns — at anytime, anywhere in the territory — to open. Okpik and other councillors persuaded Stu Hodgson to exercise that authority in Resolute Bay, where they kept the local bar open until four in the morning, two hours past the regular last call. "After that, they rescinded that one," Okpik said.

From Yellowknife, Okpik moved on to work as a municipal administrator at Spence Bay, a small settlement in the central Arctic. Then came Project Surname, which was "a big headache. I'm lucky I didn't go insane."

Okpik went to all 32 Inuit communities in the Northwest Territories and recorded everybody's family name. He spent three months in larger centres such as Frobisher Bay, one month in smaller communities such as Igloolik. It took two years altogether. In a pamphlet distributed to the communities in 1970, Okpik described his task: "You may call the Commissioner any name you like but you have to say his surname before anyone knows who you are talking about... In other parts of Canada, everybody has a family name they are known by. They do not need numbers to say who they are. We would like to know you by a name and give you a birth certificate identifying you like every other Canadian. If you have a family name, we will not need to issue numbers any more."

The problem was that many Inuit did not have family names. Traditionally, they had only one given name. Okpik suggested that, when choosing a surname, "you may want to counsel with family and relatives and ask for your grandfather's or grandmother's name. You can choose any relative's name provided you all agree on the name and the way to spell it." Not all families could agree on a name, however, and even now in any given Inuit community there may be three brothers all with different last names, or relatives with the same names but with different spellings.

There was the occasional complaint, usually from students, that people were given the wrong name. "I didn't change any names. That was a mistake when people said that," Okpik said rather defensively. "They just told me how to spell it or what it's supposed to mean. I told every student that you can go to the Justice of the Peace and change it to anything you want any time after you're nineteen years old."

After Okpik compiled lists of Inuit family names, a magistrate went to each community and held mass registrations. Okpik then gave out birth certificates with people's names rather than numbers. "Some of the old timers come up to me now and tell me they still have the card with their name on that I gave them." Yet at the time, many elders did not want to surrender their numbers. "They were getting their old age pensions, so they thought what the hell, why bother," said Okpik, who had to assure them that the cheques would still arrive after they had names.

Pressure to do away with the disc numbers came from the youth in such places as Frobisher Bay, where there was a growing white population. Inuit students were tired of answering their numbers at roll call while the white kids answered their names. They were glad to get rid of the humiliating "dog tags," as they all called the discs. The young people could not understand why they needed the disc numbers, and Okpik had to take time on his community visits to explain its paternalistic origins.

It was a long story. The Mounties historically registered births and deaths, and kept population records in the North. A Mountie of Ukrainian descent might hear an Inuit name such as "Illungiayuk" or "Ningeocheak" and try to spell it the best he could. But the French priest would spell it differently, the English medical doctor's spelling would be different again, and the Scottish fur trader would write it yet another way. Nobody in Ottawa knew who was who.

The problem was compounded when the missionaries preferred baptising natives with bibical names. Almost everyone took on a baptismal name, often with modifications so they could be pronounced in Inuktitut. Suddenly, many people were named Paulossie, Markusi, Lucasi, Joanasi. The Inuit accepted the baptismal names, but they continued to use their original Inuit names as well. Abe Okpik's father was known as Okpik, but the missionaries gave him the name "Allen." All of Abe's brothers and sisters have Allen as their surnames "because it was easier for the RCMP to write Allen than it was to write Okpik," Abe said. He got Okpik because the Mountie who registered his birth in 1929 happened to be one of a few who cared and was interested in the people of the North.

By the 1930s, the federal government considered introducing a system of identifying the Inuit. Bureaucrats thought of everything from fingerprinting every Inuk (which was tried on an experimental basis) to issuing them dog tags. One government report in 1940 recommended against the tags because: "a) Indians do not wear them; b) Misunderstandings might easily arise if Eskimos wore chains; and c) So far as we know, wards of other Dominions do not wear identification discs."

Several doctors and anthropologists who had worked closely with the Inuit suggested introducing the white man's binominal system of names. But the government decided an identification disc with a number stamped on it would suffice. Fibre discs were issued to every Inuk during the 1941 decennial census. There were problems from the start. Many Inuit threw away their discs. Hospitals and RCMP detachments ran out of them, and so many infants were born without a number. And when Family Allowance was introduced in 1945, it was realized that the disc numbers had not been matched with the Vital Statistics records. So a new set of identification discs was issued.

A numbering system was based on a district designation (three western and nine eastern) and an individual identifier. E7-4382, for example, or Abe Okpik's W3-554. The Inuit eventually accepted the discs, and artists even found the numbers convenient for marking soapstone carvings.

By the mid 1960s, some Inuit had taken on surnames. But federal bureaucrats still thought it necessary to use identification numbers to avoid "an unacceptable level of confusion." A memo written in 1966 by the Ottawa-based administrator of the Arctic, said: "At Pangnirtung, six families have taken the surname of Kilabuk while eight families are known by the surname of Kooneilusee and six families are known by the surname of Akpaliapik. We also have run into the problem of a number of people from one settlement with the same Christian name and surname who are approximately the same age. When there are three Annie Kilabuks living at Pangnirtung, Northwest Territories, the only positive means of identification is the identification number. In the South when there are three or more Annie Smiths living in one community, each person is identified by their street address, telephone number, place of employment, etc."

The use of disc numbers was not officially discontinued until the summer of 1971 when Project Surname was completed. For his work, Okpik received the Order of Canada.

With everyone named, Okpik returned to Frobisher Bay and taught Inuktitut at the high school for four years. He revisited the western Northwest Territories in 1975 and translated into Inuktitut daily radio and weekly television reports from the Mackenzie Valley Pipeline Inquiry, better known as the Berger Inquiry after its commissioner, Justice Thomas Berger. Okpik met many people in the Dene villages during the two years of community hearings throughout the Mackenzie River valley. After each hearing, the Dene would have a feast and a drum dance. "I can still hear those drums sometimes, as if they were here," Okpik said.

After the inquiry, he returned to Frobisher Bay again, and jumped from job to job, his employers including the Public Service Commission, Dome Petroleum, Esso Resources and Nanisivik Mines. Bearing the title of community liaison officer, he travelled to Inuit communities and explained what his employer of the time was doing in the Arctic. Okpik also tried to re-enter politics. He ran unsuccessfully for the Conservatives in the 1979 federal election, and lost a bid for a seat in the legislature in the 1983 territorial election.

But Okpik was getting tired of being a human suitcase. He had been to every community in the Northwest Territories, except Snowdrift, a Dene community on the east arm of Great Slave Lake. ("Though I think I'll go there someday, if somebody wants to sponsor me.") His marriage of fourteen years had fallen apart and he was getting old. He could not handle the bumpy and noisy bush planes the way he used to. So, in 1987, at the age of fifty-eight, he went back to school to take a counselling course at Arctic College in Frobisher Bay. He had received only three years of schooling back in the 1930s. Life taught him a lot, but nothing as strange as his sociology and anthropology studies at college. "When you learn you come from a chromosome and you go talk to another elder about it, he might throw you out. He'll think it's a bunch of bullshit."

When he finished his course, Okpik went to work as a counsellor (for elders) at a community social services centre. Through the elders, he found a new mission. "The elders are going to gain momentum. We're not dying off the way we were at one time. Before we were never really recognized as people. We just stayed at home and did nothing, and nobody bothered with us. But nobody writes us off anymore."

Okpik does not travel much now, just the odd trip to the Mackenzie Delta to visit his brothers and sisters. His counselling job keeps him at Iqaluit. Okpik has called this place home since the early 1960s because, for no other reason, it was where he usually came when he finished a job elsewhere. But, really, home to the former number W3-554 is the entire Northwest Territories.

DENENDEH
A Dene Celebration

RENÉ FUMOLEAU: CRITICISM AND CATHOLICISM

Father René Fumoleau came north with a paternalistic attitude towards native people, but he ended up winning a level of trust and respect from the Dene that is rarely achieved by a white man.

After working and living with the Dene for almost twenty years, the Oblate priest from France came to realize that his Church was not necessarily their Church. Since then, Fumoleau has become one of the North's leading critics of the Roman Catholic Church. "The Catholic Church is not part of the Dene culture," he said. "We may use caribou-skin drums in the church or celebrate mass in Dogrib or in Slavey, and the Dene people are coming to Mass and they are more or less listening to what the priest says, but I don't think there is fruitful dialogue between the Dene and the Church." He warns the Church had better change or it will die in the North.

A small, thin man with horn-rimmed glasses, Fumoleau wears buttoned shirts rather than the priest's collar and vestments. He is quiet, but not shy. He will give his opinion about anything and everything, when asked. He is often asked. The Dene have invited him to participate in their political discussions, research their history, photograph their lives, and lecture about them across the country. He has tried, perhaps more than anyone, to bridge the gap between native spirituality and the Catholic faith.

He was not always such a staunch defender of native people. At first, he was not much different from any other pioneer of the Catholic faith who had come to the region in the past 150 years. Born in France, he was ordained a priest with the congregation of the Oblates of Mary Immaculate in 1952 and the following year, at the age of twenty-seven, he was made the parish priest at Fort Good Hope, a Dene community on the Mackenzie River, just below the Arctic Circle. "I figured that these people were extremely happy to see me, even if they had never invited me and didn't know that I was coming. I didn't come with the mentality that there was something for me to learn. I came to teach them. I don't even think I came with an open mind. Sure, I learned the language and travelled like the people did, but that was not really to learn. That was to help them understand what I wanted to tell."

The Church did do some good. Mission hospitals saved lives and even entire villages when the Dene were suffering from tuberculosis and lack of food. Missionaries developed writing systems for aboriginal languages and educated the people who are now the North's political leaders. However, to this day many native people have bitter memories of the Church's attempts to eradicate native culture. In particular, they have not forgotten the Church's policy of separating children from their families and sending them to residential schools where, after learning how to write their language, the natives were punished for speaking it rather than English or French. "It was awful in those days," Fumoleau admitted. "I remember the young girls coming home from school with their hair dyed light brown and their faces were powdered white to look like white people. The old people cried when these kids came back from school."

Instead of working to help maintain native culture, the Church taught the Dene to adapt to western civilization and paved the way for big government and big business to move into the North. It even helped implement government policies, such as persuading the natives to sign the early treaties. The advance of civilization culminated in 1967, when the administration of government services in the North was moved from Ottawa to Yellowknife. The Mackenzie River Valley was invaded by government administrators, technicians, game wardens, development officers and the like. The entire Dene world fell apart as the chiefs and elders lost their authority over the communities. "The kids were told not to listen to the old-timers. They were told to go to school, to listen to the modern world and forget the past. It was told in really a disgusting way, so bluntly," recalled Fumoleau.

The same year, the government sent a floating museum, complete with a ferris wheel and a children's amusement park, down the Mackenzie River to commemorate the Canadian centennial. So nobody would miss the celebration, the government flew people living inland to communities along the river. It was the first time the Dene had met together in large groups. They started to talk and exchange ideas and, in one summer, the North changed. The consciousness of the people was raised and by 1969 the Indian Brotherhood, now called the Dene Nation, was formed to represent the political interests of the Dene.

In 1970, "by good luck or by grace," Fumoleau was sent to the government centre of Yellowknife. It was a time when the Dene were organizing and northern politics was boiling over. There were tensions between the native groups and the governments and businesses, and racism between Dene and white people. Since a parish priest already worked in Yellowknife, the bishop told Fumoleau to "see what you can do with the Indians."

"I guess in my mind and the bishop's mind, I was to follow the same ministry pattern of teaching kids and providing sacraments," Fumoleau said. "The established order was supposed to last forever, then suddenly the situation changed. Everything that was secure before was now up in the air and the people were asking for something else, for a different kind of ministry."

Fumoleau was affected by the new atmosphere — he became an enthusiastic champion of native people. His "conversion" took place in the midst of his work, as he learned first hand about the Dene traditional lifestyle and researched their history. It was facilitated, he thinks now, by the fact that he had not been born in Canada. "Every Canadian is raised with the mentality that they know that the Indians are good for nothing, that they haven't done anything good so far, and that they are lazy and dirty. We didn't have those kinds of suspicions in Europe. For us, the Indians were still the noble savages with feathered bonnets and galloping on horses on the prairies. White Canadians have the same ideas about Indians as the French have towards the North Africans. I know it would be very difficult for me even now to work with North African people because of what I learned 60 years ago when I was a kid."

In 1971, Dene leaders asked Fumoleau to research the old Indian treaties their forefathers had signed with the federal government — Treaty 8 in 1900 and Treaty 11 in 1921. What the Dene had in mind was a bit of digging in the Catholic mission archives. Fumoleau ended up spending two years searching through the government archives in Ottawa and the Hudson's Bay Company's files in Winnipeg. He produced a 400-page published book about the modern history of the Dene. It was dedicated to "the youngest Indian child in the Northwest Territories."

By the mid 1970s most Churches were voicing support for the efforts of aboriginal organizations to have native rights placed before the demands of resource development. Fumoleau himself began delivering speeches across the country for Project North, an ecumenical group formed to publicize the native peoples' struggle for justice. For that purpose, he put together a 16 mm film, called "I Was Born Here." It was made from 250 of his photographs, which he had started taking in 1967. That year he was going to visit his mother in France and realized he did not have a single picture to show her the place where he had already spent fifteen years. So he bought a camera and shot seven or eight rolls of film. Twenty years and 8,000 slides later, he has become a renowned northern photographer who has captured the Dene and their culture on film more than anyone. His photographs have graced the pages of books, magazines and calendars. "Photography helped me a great deal to reflect on myself and the people," he said. "It forced me to slow down; to take pictures and understand people. And it had a lot of value for the Dene — their way of life was worth recording."

Fumoleau was in his mid-forties when his attitude towards the Dene changed. He was then young compared to many other priests in the North, and today, in his sixties, he is still one of the youngest priests.

The Catholic Church in the North is faced with an aging and dwindling priesthood. The Mackenzie Diocese had seventy-five priests when Fumoleau arrived in 1953. There were thirty-five in 1988. A fresh batch of younger, indigenous priests is nowhere in sight. Unlike the Anglican Church in the eastern Arctic, where half the ministers are Inuit, the Roman Catholic Church has had only two native priests in the Mackenzie Valley, and both are now dead. The vow of celibacy that the Catholic Church requires of its priests is largely to blame, claim some Dene leaders. Culturally, a man who is not married with a family is considered a failure in native society.

Fumoleau, however, doesn't think that celibacy is the root cause of the church's difficulties. The problem runs deeper. He feels that more native people would participate if the Church were more in tune with their society and if they could play a role in the institution's decision-making.

The Catholic church claims it stands side by side with the disadvantaged and poor people of the world, but it failed miserably in 1984, when the Pope was scheduled to visit Fort Simpson as part of a

Canadian tour. His plane could not land because of fog. The Pope wanted to wait until the fog lifted, but Church and government bureaucrats decided to carry on so John Paul would be on time for the next stop — Ottawa. That was when Father Fumoleau said: "Today, I'm ashamed to be a Catholic.

"I was so mad to find out that the Church is no different than any political or business organization. It has the same standards and the same values."

Fumoleau felt better about his Church in 1987 when the Pope returned to the North and celebrated mass for a gathering of 5,000 native people at Fort Simpson. "When you have that many people together, a lot of things happen. There's a lot of talking, a lot of reflection. There was a lot of respect for the Pope as a spiritual leader. People thought of him as one of their elders. The Pope gave them confidence that they can make it. After all the struggles of the past fifteen years, the Pope came along and said 'go ahead, you're on the right track.' He said to the Dene that they're not a bunch of silly people after all. The Pope was sitting on the podium with four aboriginal leaders and he was listening to them. He didn't come to teach and to make any pronouncement. He came to listen to the people."

Although he was qualified, Fumoleau was not considered for the post when a new bishop for the Mackenzie was selected in 1986. He had had too many differences with some Church administrators. Comments aimed at the Church by Fumoleau and others were "hard to take," Bishop Paul Piche said before he retired. "They showed an ignorance in judging in terms of today what was done 150 years ago. We did then what we thought was best at that time."

"I don't mind criticizing the Church," Fumoleau said. "I think there's a place for self-criticism in any organization. We cannot say that nothing should be criticized because we are the Church. The Church is human. If Christ trusted people to run the Church, then He was expecting there would be some mistakes."

Any organization that does not criticize itself "is in a danger of disappearing," he insisted. It has to recognize what is wrong and steer a different course. It is time for the Catholic Church in the North to change direction. Without the prospect of recruiting new clergymen, neither from outside nor within the North, "we have to discuss and redefine the various ministries needed in the Church."

Priests performed much more than religious duties before government moved north. But as responsibility for health care and education passed, so did the need for a large priesthood. Furthermore, a large percentage of a priest's current functions could be done by other people. There are plans to establish a corps of lay preachers and counsellors in each Dene community. Different people would baptize children, lead services, give religious teachings, organize celebrations, marry couples and preside at funerals. The role of the priest would be first to act as a unifying force in the local community. "These things have been done in other places. In Africa and South America, this new vision of the Church is not a vision anymore. I met a priest in Peru with a parish of 135,000 people and the whole parish was divided into seventy-five mini parishes," Fumoleau said.

"But really," he admitted, "I don't know what's going to happen to the Church in the North. That's why I feel hopeful. I think it's beautiful because everything is possible. I think that's the way a Church should be. We have to go in faith."

Fumoleau's own future, as he approaches retirement age, is as uncertain as his Church's. He is content living in a small house with no plumbing in a district of Yellowknife where the average house sells for a quarter of a million dollars. He drives around the neighbourhood in an old pick-up truck with a bumper sticker that reads: "One nuclear bomb can ruin your whole day." He does a little research and writing and a lot of visiting and counselling. He holds seminars and workshops for any group from the Dene Nation to the Mennonite community in Toronto, on subjects ranging from aboriginal rights and native history to Christian attitudes towards the environment. He may continue doing all this, or he may return to a small community and retire in the local old folks' home.

When Fumoleau first arrived at Fort Good Hope, there was an old man who used to sit on the river bank for hours on end. One day the young priest built up enough courage to ask him why he sat there all day. "Jowida," the elder replied, which roughly translates from Slavey as "I am here," meaning, in effect, that "I'm at peace with myself. This is the right place and I'm the right person to be here."

Thirty-five years later, Fumoleau thought "maybe it's time for me to do what the old man was saying — go sit on the river bank and feel comfortable with myself... but at the same time, I've accumulated a lot of experience and knowledge and it's my responsibility to share it with other people." Faith will once again have to take its course.

BENJAMIN ARREAK: ALTERNATIVE ANGLICANISM

The Anglican Church in the North is in a state of transition. British-born Anglican missionaries, who sailed to the Arctic with Scottish whalers near the end of the nineteenth century, converted the Inuit from Shamanism. They and their successors spent the next 100 years further convincing the Inuit that the Anglicans, not the French-born Catholic priests, spoke the truth about God.

The progress they made in this direction is evident in the fact that by 1989 over half of the thirty-three priests of the Diocese of the Arctic were Inuit. At the same time, however, their success had an unintended side effect. Many of the Inuit minorities in the North today are presenting a view of Christianity that is markedly different from that of the missionaries.

The first Inuit deacon ordained in Canada was Armand Tagoona, of the Keewatin region, in 1959. But the conscious decision to train indigenous ministers came a decade later with a shortage of clergy across the Arctic. In 1970, the Anglican Church set up the Arthur Turner Training School, named after an early Anglican missionary. The school was located in Pangnirtung on Baffin Island because that was where the Church had some empty buildings. Michael Gardener, who had been running a catechist training school in nearby Cape Dorset, started up the new theology college. The first group of students were six older Inuit catechists or lay readers who had been involved in church activities for many years. The second class, in 1972, consisted of four young, bright, brash and bilingual Inuit who were more or less persuaded to attend the school by their local minister or the bishop himself. Among them was twenty-five-year-old Benjamin Arreak.

"Ben was a real, shall we say, seeking student," Gardener recalled. "He was like a dog with a bone. He chewed and chewed and got as much as possible out of it."

Arreak felt he had to make up for lost time. Born in Pond Inlet in 1947, he had not gone to church as a youth because there was never one to attend. His father worked for the RCMP as a special native constable at various remote outpost settlements on Ellesmere Island. At Alexandra Fiord, which was as close to the North Pole as any existing community, the Arreaks were one of just two families. The head of the other family was also a special constable. Realizing the absurdity of the situation after seven years, the government shut down the station and Arreak's father was transferred to Cape Christian, a United States Coast Guard base on the east coast of Baffin Island. There Benjamin learned to speak some English "as the Americans and policemen did not speak Eskimo."

In 1966, after six years at the base, he married and went on a six-day, 350-mile "honeymoon" journey by dog sled north to Pond Inlet. He worked there as a heavy equipment operator and climbed the local government ranks to become the secretary-manager of the municipality. "During these busy days I really felt that I was looking for something else that I could not understand and something that might be a little bigger than the job I was doing," he said. "I knew that something was going on in my heart but I did not know quite what to do about it."

Arreak started to go to church because it was a good place to socialize. Northerners attend church more than people in southern Canada partially because there is not much else to do in their small, isolated communities, Arreak said. "If you didn't go to church, you would be seen as different from the others, not normal."

Soon Arreak was helping with the services and teaching Sunday school to the children. "More and more I felt God was calling me to his ministry but I thought it was impossible for me to enter because I did not really know English and had never attended school. In other words, I found it an easy excuse to do nothing." With encouragement from the local minister and an invitation from the bishop, Arreak went to the clergy training school. The school has since evolved into an academic theology college with a full-time principal, but when Arreak attended from 1972 to 1975, Gardener was both the principal and the local parish priest. As a result, the students received a lot of practical training at the church. "It was almost like learning on the job, especially on Sundays," Arreak said. The classes were taught mostly in Inuktitut, which Gardener spoke fluently. There were also English grammar lessons, which Arreak found difficult. "My English even right now is not that good."

After his ordination in 1975, Arreak was appointed to his first parish — Salluit, in northern Quebec. Life there was not easy at first. The Inuit parishioners did not believe that one of their own could hold the most respected position in the community. They also objected both to Arreak's introduction of such practices as guitar-playing and hand-clapping, and to his view that a person could belong to another denomination and still be a Christian. When he first expressed his ecumenical views, the congregation was deeply offended. "They got really mad at me and told me that I wasn't an Anglican. They tried to get me to leave the settlement."

The problem was simple, Arreak explained. "After all those years of having white clergymen, the Inuit believe things that aren't really accurate. Anglicanism is the only thing they have ever known. When they start to hear the real truth, they don't agree at first because they have never heard it before. They think you're trying to destroy their beliefs."

Yet Arreak had one advantage over white clergymen — because he was an Inuk, he spoke the language and knew the culture. He could talk directly to the people, "to their hearts." Initially his style shocked them, but after a while they grew used to him. By the time he was ready to leave Salluit, the people were asking him to stay. In the community of 700 people he left behind one of northern Quebec's four self-supporting native parishes, where the local church rather than the diocese looked after its affairs and hired the priest.

From 1980 to the present, Arreak has served the parish of Pangnirtung. His services now are almost always in Inuktitut. The Book of Common Prayer and hymnbook have been translated into Inuktitut, but Arreak has to improvise with alternative prayers and the baptismal service. As for the Bible, missionaries had translated it over one hundred years ago when they were introducing a syllabic writing system to the Inuit, who until then had an entirely oral language. By Arreak's time, however, the translation was out of date, inaccurate and contained spelling errors. "Everytime we have a worship, we have to hand out corrections before we start."

But this will soon change. In 1978, the United Bible Society decided to translate the Bible into all languages of the world. Four Inuit ministers were chosen for the Inuktitut translation, two for each testament. Three of the four translators were graduates of the Arthur Turner school's class of '75. Arreak works on the New Testament. It is a formidable job, for literal translation of the standard King James Version is not sufficient. When the English-language Bible refers to somebody speaking, it often uses the expression, "he opened his mouth." In Inuktitut, "that doesn't mean anything. Your mouth is always open. The opening on your face is already there, you don't have to cut it open again," Arreak said. "Our language is more practical than English. We don't really have words for abstract things. You cannot translate into Inuktitut words like 'grace' and 'blessing' and 'peace.'"

Translations depend on the context. To say "world peace," Arreak would write "there is no war" in Inuktitut. To describe the angel telling Mary, "Peace be with you," he would write "Do not be afraid." On the other hand, a concept such as man's inner peace is not a problem because the Inuit have a word for it.

The Inuit used the Revised Standard and New International versions for the translation, and the simpler and less structured Good News Bible for a model to divide the passages into verses and subject sections. "We don't want to get away from the exact content, but at the same time we have to be simple and use words that everybody will understand," Arreak explained. Although the Inuit share the same language, there are about a dozen regional dialects. An explanation of "peace" in one dialect may not work in another. "Sometimes we just use the one word that most people understand and use footnotes or a word list for the others."

The first draft of the Inuktitut Bible was completed in 1986. After checking, proof-reading and re-writing, the final version is expected to be published in 1990. Arreak works on the bible translation in the mornings and takes care of his parish duties in the afternoon.

Arreak prefers the translation work. He admits he is "not really a good preacher. I feel nervous every time I'm at the pulpit. Whenever I hear others up there, I think they are stronger speakers. I consider myself more effective when I'm counselling people. When you counsel, you have more direct contact. If they don't understand you, they can stop you. When you're preaching in the church, you can be talking and talking and talking, but you don't get any response and the people listening to you might not really care about what you're saying."

By 1988, after eight years in Pangnirtung, Arreak was finding his parish work at the St. Luke's Church somewhat frustrating and tedious.

"I might not be the right kind of person for that town," he said. He remains open to suggestions, although he has already turned down two invitations from the parish at Pond Inlet. The Church does not think it a good idea for a clergyman to return to preach in his home community. "Your effectiveness would be limited because the people have known you from the beginning. They know how you grew up, how you used to be. Especially with relatives, it can be difficult when you go into deeper things, when they go through a difficult period or when someone has died. It's too close. It's almost like a doctor. A doctor can't treat his own family. Also, looking at the biblical side, Jesus said that a prophet is never respected in his home town."

All Churches in the North have been accused of paternalism towards the natives. They taught the native people to accept the cultural and religious values of white society and, while they gave them tasks in the church such as being lay readers and catechists, they never put them in positions of real leadership. The Anglican was the first, and some say the only, Church to allow the native people to have a say in the direction of their faith. The Anglicans' success is judged by the number of aboriginal clergymen compared to other denominations. In 1988, there were twenty Inuit Anglican ministers in the eastern Arctic. There was not one aboriginal priest in the western Northwest Territories, where the Dene Indians are predominantly Roman Catholic.

The requirement of celibacy may be the reason there are so few native Catholic priests, said Arreak. But, he added, that requirement in itself demonstrates an underlying attitude that native people should adapt to the ways of the Church rather than the Church adapt to native culture. Most aboriginal people grow up in large families and they are expected to raise many children themselves. Arreak has six brothers and six sisters, and so far seven children, and two grandchildren, with more certainly to come.

The marriage question aside, "the Anglicans started to believe and trust the native people right from the beginning, when people started to adopt Christianity as a religion," Arreak argued. Services conducted in Inuktitut and altars draped in sealskins are symbols that the Inuit culture is alive within the church. During a royal visit to Frobisher Bay (now called Iqaluit) in 1970, the national newspaper columnist Charles Lynch noted: "It is doubted if the Queen in all her years of official church going, has ever attended a service of such simplicity, such deep sincerity. Throughout the proceedings a husky dog wandered about, receiving the occasional pat from Her Majesty and Prince Philip."

Many native clergymen, Arreak included, have worked to influence the Church administration and policies through national Church conferences and meetings. Yet there has been divisions among the native people over how far they should go. Some Indian tribes, the Cree in particular, have pushed for radical changes to the Church. They have sought an all-native ministry in their homelands and an acceptance of traditional spiritual rituals involving sweat lodges (a purification rite that involves exposing participants to fire or steam in a small hut) and the burning of sweetgrass. Arreak finds "it difficult to agree with some of those Cree people. Even some of the Cree clergymen are not strong Christians. Some of them still seem to be mixed up in the old spirituality. I think it's because the Cree feel they have been neglected and ignored by the whites and the Church. The Inuit were never deeply hurt, so we don't have that problem with racism."

Almost none of the Inuit in the eastern Arctic openly believes in the old spiritual ways. Arreak has heard stories of "underground" shamans, "but to me, it's just like stories and legends."

The Cree have tried to organize conferences of only native priests. The Inuit ministers have always refused to participate because, they tell the Cree, they have different goals. "I don't think the goal is for all ministers to be Inuit," Arreak said. "We're not like the Indian people. We don't look to the future and say that all clergymen should be native. We want the Inuit people and the white people to work together, that is our goal. It really doesn't matter if the minister is an Inuit person or a white person, so long as he has been called by God."

PART II
POLITICAL LIVES

NICK SIBBESTON: FILIBUSTERING IN SLAVEY

The only thing Nick Sibbeston ever used to wear was a beaded buckskin vest.

The Metis member of the Northwest Territories legislature went to work one day in 1982, removed his jacket and tie and revealed an open collar and a tanned vest embroidered by Dene weavers. That was what his constituents in Fort Simpson wore, he reasoned, so that was what he was going to wear while representing them in the legislature.

After that, the Speaker of the House, dressed in the traditional British Parliamentary vestment, occasionally would try to enforce the established dress code and tell Sibbeston to put on a neck tie. Sibbeston would reply: "Only if you take off that silly black robe."

Sibbeston was a determined, some say stubborn, politician with an unpredictable temper. During a debate in 1981, he said that he was almost in tears because Inuit MLAs were not taking a motion of his very seriously.

"Go ahead and cry," taunted Tagak Curley, one of the Inuit members.

"You better watch it. I'm going to give you a punch," said Sibbeston, who then walked two seats down the assembly bench and landed a heavy blow to the side of Curley's head. He returned to his place and the speaker told him to leave the legislature for the rest of the day.

"You can drag me out," Sibbeston muttered, but he then left voluntarily.

In another fit of rage a month later, Sibbeston hurled a coffee cup across the floor of the legislative chambers and shouted: "You can stick this fuckin' legislature!" He stormed out of the assembly, leaving its occupants in stunned silence.

The flying cup was intended for Pete Fraser, the deputy speaker and chairman of the legislative committee-of-the-whole, who had refused to hear a debate on the plight of native people. With the mug lying shattered on the floor, Fraser broke the stillness: "I've heard those statements two or three times before and I don't want to listen to them again." He then carried on to the next item of business. Shaking in anger outside the chambers, Sibbeston told reporters that even though the majority of the MLAs were native, the Northwest Territories government did not represent the Dene and was not worthy of support. He claimed that native people could not understand why the government keeps selling them liquor when it was destroying so many lives, why renowned hunters were not qualified for jobs as local game wardens, and why people who spoke only their aboriginal language could not communicate with their government. He said that he was resigning his seat. He later reconsidered.

Sibbeston also brought the assembly to a halt by filibustering in the Dene language of Slavey, which he spoke as fluently as English. Soon the government hired a translator to interpret Sibbeston's words into English. When asked how long he would be around, the interpreter said, "I don't know; as long as Nick needs me, I guess."

By the mid 1980s, not only was a Slavey interpreter still around, but there was a growing forty-person interpreter corps providing simultaneous translation in the legislature of all of the Northwest Territories' seven aboriginal languages. And the assembly modified its dress code to allow traditional native wardrobe alongside the three-piece suits. Further recognition of the native presence, such as the Inuit wall hangings, seal skins and beaver pelts, caribou-skin drums, moosehair tuftings and beadwork that had come to decorate the legislature walls, was also largely due to Sibbeston's tactics.

When twenty-seven-year-old Sibbeston was elected for the first time in 1970, the legislature consisted of appointed and elected members who had little power. The government was run as an Ottawa colony and the legislature was merely a debating society to which the federally appointed commissioner would listen on occasion and at his leisure. It would be another decade before the Territories had an entirely elected legislature representing all its peoples, and it would be 1986 before all of the territorial government's decisions were made exclusively by elected representatives.

Sibbeston quit the legislature after his first term. He went to the University of Alberta law school and became the first northern native lawyer. His law career amounted to practising a brief two years in Yellowknife. He entered politics, again, in 1979, and in 1983 was made a cabinet minister. As the minister responsible for local government, Sibbeston joined a 1984 Dene boycott of the opening ceremonies for a Mackenzie Valley pipeline, even though other Northwest Territories ministers attended and the government officially supported the project. The following year, concerned that the territorial government might revert back to its old ways when natives had no control over matters such as oil and gas development, Sibbeston decided to put his name forward to become the government leader. The legislature had ousted the previous leader, Richard Nerysoo, and a cabinet shuffle left just two native ministers — Sibbeston and Tagak Curley — on the eight-member executive. Nerysoo, a Dene from the Mackenzie River delta, had received national recognition two years earlier when he became the first aboriginal to lead a government in Canada. Sibbeston felt it was important to continue the trend. "Being such a person, I thought I had a responsibility to give it a try."

The Northwest Territories' twenty-four MLAs are all elected as independents and not as members of any particular political party. Together they choose the cabinet and government leader. The only ministers interested in the leader's job in 1985 were Sibbeston and Dennis Patterson, a white lawyer from Iqaluit, on Baffin Island. That there were more MLAs from the western Northwest Territories than the eastern part, and that there were more natives than whites, worked to Sibbeston's advantage. The man who had rubbed every colleague the wrong way at least once was elected to lead them all.

Sibbeston never made many political allies across the North and he did not have much of a honeymoon with the voters. When told over the telephone that Sibbeston was the new government leader, Rhoda Innuksuk, the president of the Inuit Tapirisat of Canada, said, "You're kidding! You're kidding! I need some time to think about this," and then hung up.

"I personally am a little uneasy... no, very uneasy" about Sibbeston as government leader, said Roger Gruben, an Inuvialuit (western Arctic Inuit) leader and, at the time, the chairman of the Nunavut Constitutional Forum, an organization trying to set up a new territory above the treeline. "Because of his past statements, people are skeptical that he can represent their interests fairly."

Sibbeston and Gruben had clashed before. Sibbeston had been the chairman of the Western Constitutional Forum, which was negotiating (with Gruben's group) a boundary line to divide the Territories. In that position, Sibbeston travelled to Inuvialuit communities around the Beaufort Sea and insisted they had no choice but to be included in the western territory after the division. He suggested that the Inuvialuit, who were in a dilemma over which side to join, would not be able to go to hospitals and schools in the West if the Beaufort Sea became part of the Nunavut territory. When he became government leader, Sibbeston resigned from the Constitutional Forum and said he would no longer involve himself in the debate over division. Gruben was skeptical: "As they say, the proof is in the pudding; we will be watching his performance carefully."

Sibbeston was quick to a make his mark as government leader. He took a swipe at Yellowknife, home of the northern establishment since 1967 when the federal government made a capital city out of what was then a small gold mining town on the north shore of Great Slave Lake. By the 1980s, Yellowknife had grown into a modern city with office towers and expensive restaurants. One-quarter of the Northwest Territories' 50,000 residents live in the capital city, most of them transient government employees from the South. Other Northerners, Nick Sibbeston included, envied and resented Yellowknife's amenities. The city was "no different from the South" and it had better start reflecting the people of the entire Territories, or else "you may see people talk about setting up a new capital," Sibbeston said. "The city must do things like adopt native names for its buildings, streets and developments." He offered the mayor and aldermen "good free advice" on how to become a truly northern city. To cover the costs for replacing street signs, "if they want money, we'll give them money."

City councillors told the government to keep its advice and money; they were not going to change any names. After presenting a long list of Yellowknife landmarks named after native people, including Matonabee Street after the chief who guided Samuel Hearne across the Arctic, the council said that preference was not given to any particular cultural group when it came to streets and avenues. "It is not all native or all white, but a place for all of us," said Deputy Mayor Pat McMahon, noting Dagenais Drive was named after an Italian pianist.

Sibbeston's political career had always been coloured with symbolic rhetoric, but once in power he was better able to turn his words into action. He turfed out much of the senior civil service — the "old boys network" and the "Baffin mafia" (in reference to those who started government careers in the 1960s as administrators on Baffin Island) who had been running the government in the authoritative style of the former commissioner. "Nobody is secure just because they've been a civil servant for twenty years," Sibbeston declared.

He told surviving civil servants that their "allegiances, whole lives, all their energies should go to helping the people... That is the way their efforts will be recognized; they are no longer working for a bunch of people in Yellowknife." He wished to imply that elected representatives were now in charge, but bureaucrats interpreted his comments to mean that they could now ignore established government policies and orders from above if they thought they were not popular with some people in some communities. "Threats that public servants must be responsive to the people and not to their bosses makes me more convinced than ever that I'm living in Cuckoo-land," said Brian Lewis, who started working for the government in 1963 as a school principal in the Inuit community of Cape Dorset and rose to become deputy minister of education. He was elected a Yellowknife MLA after the government dismissed him in 1985 because he was, according to Sibbeston, "floating around without a real certainty of what his job is."

"When a whole new group of people came into the executive (in 1983), we didn't know if we had the right to appoint our own deputy ministers. Now there is no longer any uncertainty." So said Sibbeston after he forced the deputy minister of personnel into early retirement and hired an old school chum to take his place. "I'm going to be in charge of personnel and I'm going to choose the deputy minister of my choice."

After taking over responsibility for the government's personnel department, the last portfolio held by the commissioner, Sibbeston initiated an affirmative action policy to increase the number of natives in the civil service. "We're politely shoving the commissioner out of his present role. Eventually he will open buildings, cut ribbons."

Pledging to increase the "stature and dignity" of the elected ministers at the expense of appointed officials, Sibbeston said that "ministers are going to be cared for and looked after properly with respect to basic things such as housing and travel."

The government leader's residence, which housed the appointed commissioner during the 1960s and 1970s, topped the improvement list. "The first night I slept in the house the furnace ran all night non-stop. I have never lived, in all my life, in such terrible housing. We are going to upgrade that house and make it into a fine house for a government leader to live in or future premiers to live in." The image of the government leader needed "a boost," he said. "It now is something less than the commissioner's and something more than a minister's. There's some uncertainty. He needs to act more like a provincial premier."

Sibbeston built up the government leader's office with political aides and advisors and a press secretary who was paid a salary that was about $20,000 more than any other government public relations officer with similar duties. Under Sibbeston, government in the Northwest Territories grew to resemble governments of the southern provinces. The new government leader said he would like to call himself "premier" and his executive a "cabinet," just as they did down south. "What's a government leader? What's an executive council? Particularly when I go south I have to explain what it is."

People were outraged that Sibbeston had the audacity to bestow the title of premier upon himself. They protested that a territorial government leader could not claim the same status as a provincial premier until full responsible government was achieved. Arguments that Alberta and Saskatchewan had "premiers" before the granting of provincial status mattered not. Those with long memories could not bear the thought of the mouthy Nick Sibbeston being a premier.

Sibbeston regarded the title not so much as an attempt to enhance his own personal image, but rather as another gesture to symbolize the wresting of power from Ottawa. But with the political waters boiling over, Sibbeston declined to jump in; he resigned himself to the hope that maybe some day a Northerner will be called a premier. For the first time in his political career, he accepted the fact that progress sometimes had to wait.

Sibbeston, the back-bench MLA, was considered harmless enough, but as government leader, every move was scrutinized and construed as government policy. He was upset by regular bashings from the media. He denounced the Yellowknife newspapers for being racist, claiming that he was being picked on because he was native. He said that his predecessor, Richard Nerysoo, suffered the same fate. However, Nerysoo, who had an absolutely disastrous relationship with the press, denied that he ever faced an anti-native bias. If anything, native journalists were his toughest critics. Suggesting Sibbeston get used to it, Nerysoo said: "You can't walk away from the media by saying you are a native."

Sibbeston tried keeping quiet, or at least watched what he said, after his mouth got him deep trouble at the 1986 annual conference of the Northwest Territories Native Women's Association. Addressing the issue of government support for daycare centres, he told a predominantly female audience that "if you leave your kids for someone else to look after, you're not doing your job." Daycares would make it "easy for young girls to have babies and not properly look after them. To have good people in society, good men and women, you have to bring them up properly and you don't do that by sending them to residential schools and daycare."

The media, taking into account that Sibbeston himself was raised without real family and attended residential schools for most of his youth, had a field day. Afterwards, not much was heard from the controversial and articulate renegade in the buckskin jacket. He took his seat in the legislature and sipped from a glass of water — coffee mugs had by then been disallowed. He did not participate in controversial debates. His aides and advisors and press secretary, who used to cringe every time he tossed aside a prepared speech in order to reveal what was on his mind, were elated when he started to read the non-offensive material that they had spent three days writing.

Sibbeston claimed that he no longer had to be outspoken and outlandish to force change. After a meeting with leaders of the North's French-speaking community, who were concerned that services in French would suffer as Sibbeston concentrated on accelerating the use of aboriginal languages in government, he noted: "You accomplish nothing by breaking all the china in the place. There are civil ways to handle this sort of thing."

Inuit leaders tested Sibbeston's new calm and neutrality. They denounced the territorial government's aggressive pursuit of powers from Ottawa before land claims were settled. On several occasions, Sibbeston diplomatically suggested a meeting among northern government and native leaders to discuss the matter. In a blatant attempt to frustrate Sibbeston, the Inuit repeatedly accepted invitations to such encounters, but cancelled at the last moment. "We still want to hold the meeting, but obviously we need other people to attend," Sibbeston said after one of the Inuit pull-outs. "When they're ready they'll let us know and we will have a meeting. It's no big deal."

In conversation, Sibbeston comes across as a civil and understanding man. It would be difficult to imagine him breaking china or coffee mugs. He holds strong traditional Roman Catholic values, and has difficulty approving even social drinking. His home renovations included ripping out a basement bar that previous commissioners used for entertaining guests. Sibbeston is very much a family man and spends his rare free hours at home with his wife and six children. He is a reputed master in the kitchen, and his recipe for home-made bannock is regarded as one of the finest in the Mackenzie River valley. (Mix together five cups of flour, four tablespoons of baking powder, sugar, salt, melted lard, water and raisins, and bake at 350F for twenty-five to thirty minutes.)

While trying to avoid controversy in November 1986, Sibbeston was criticized by the Dene chief in his home town of Fort Simpson for not being "bold enough" of late. Sibbeston declared that "it is lonely" at the top.

In 1987 Sibbeston easily won a re-election bid and was re-appointed to the cabinet. But when he went up against Dennis Patterson again for the leadership, he lost. Instead, Sibbeston was made the minister of economic development and tourism. Six months later it was becoming apparent that he just did not have the energy and feist of his past, and Patterson demoted him to the relatively minor portfolios of minister of government services and minister responsible for the Northwest Territories Housing Corporation.

In September 1988, to protest his demotion, he resigned from the cabinet. "I'm used to working on more exciting and more profound things," he said.

Sibbeston took a seat in the legislature on the backbench, where he had been more effective anyway. He had made his mark on northern politics. He helped turn a government run by white Southerners into one run by native Northerners. The revolution was over and he was no longer a radical.

TAGAK CURLEY: TWENTY-EIGHT WORDS LATER

On March 16, 1987, Tagak Curley emerged from the legislative chambers into a scrum of journalists. He ran his fingers through his hair.

"I'm okay," he said.

The North's most effective Inuit politician had just been dumped as minister of economic development and tourism. He lost his portfolio because of a twenty-eight-word note he had scribbled the previous week.

At issue was a mysterious $100,000 government grant given to a private business in Rankin Inlet, a town in the minister's constituency. The grant did not fall under any specific government programme and MLAs found it strange that the money would be, as one legislator put it, "hanging in the air, waiting to be plucked by someone."

While MLAs debated whether or not to strike the grant from the department's budget, Curley sent a note to a Dene legislator, Sam Gargan, who was wavering on which way he would vote. The note read: "Sam, I am not sure you need any support from the department towards any private sector in your riding if you can not support private sector in my community! Tagak."

To Gargan, the note was a threat to keep government funds from his constituency, a poor rural riding in the Mackenzie River Valley. Other MLAs claimed the note was a blatant threat to use public power as personal retribution. The day after he received the note, Gargan called for a vote of non-confidence in Curley as the minister of economic development.

"It was not a threat," Curley pleaded. "I do not believe in threats. I think threats are a sign of weakness and it was never intended to be a threat... It is unfortunate and I regret that my note caused such an overblown impression of what I meant. It was intended to give the message that one project was no different from any other project. That was what I was trying to portray. Obviously because of my lack of ability to make my point clear, it was misunderstood."

Curley spent the most agonizing weekend of his life awaiting the trial that would determine his political future. The legislature took on the appearance of a courtroom when Curley faced his prosecutors on the Monday. The government leader at the time, Nick Sibbeston, defended his minister. "Short of getting on his knees, Mr. Curley has done all he can to say he's sorry. I accept that he is truly sorry and should be forgiven." Backbenchers said he should have recognized a threat when he wrote one and that it was not good enough for ministers to do as they pleased "so long as they apologize if they get caught."

After two and a half hours of debate, Curley lost his seat by ten votes to eight, with three abstentions. Ironically, he could not command the support of other Inuit legislators. Inuit MLAs tend to vote as a bloc in the legislature and, for many years, they almost always followed Curley's lead. If there was one person responsible for organizing the Inuit and leading them into modern times, it was Tagak Curley.

He was born in 1944 in a tent on the barrenlands of Southampton Island, in northern Hudson Bay. He grew up in a family with sixteen brothers and sisters, all of whom lived as nomads, moving seasonally in search of game. When Tagak was eight years old, his family was forced to move to a community that the federal government set up and called Coral Harbour. He went to school, in the North and the South, and learned English. For a short while he drove a front-end loader and other heavy equipment in Coral Harbour for the Ministry of Transport. Learning a different language and earning an hourly wage were his introduction to a strange, new way of life.

Tagak Curley, the politician, was born after working for the Department of Indian Affairs and Northern Development for four years in the late 1960s. He was employed to improve adult education and develop economic co-operatives in Inuit communities. As a middle man between Ottawa and the Inuit, Curley came to realize that the Inuit had little say in the decision-making process of government. He quit his job and began his career as a "political activist." In 1970, when he was twenty-six years old, Curley became the founding president of the Inuit Tapirisat of Canada. The Tapirisat, formed to represent the political, economic and cultural interests of Canada's 20,000 Inuit, set out to make Canada aware of the Inuit and the Inuit aware of Canada. It launched negotiations with Ottawa to settle Inuit land claims, which were closely linked with a proposal to create a new territory in the eastern Arctic. Envisioned was an Inuit homeland to be called Nunavut, meaning "our land" in Inuktitut. After steering the activities of the Inuit Tapirisat for four years, Curley moved on to the prominent positions of executive director of the Inuit Cultural Institute, from 1975 to 1983, and president of Nunasi Corporation, the Inuit business arm, from 1979 to 1983. He was first elected to the legislative assembly in 1979, representing communities of the Keewatin region along the west coast of Hudson Bay. He was re-elected in 1983 and was appointed to the executive council.

The vote to remove Curley from office marked an end to Curley's two-decade long dominance of Inuit politics. Other Inuit now had matured politically, and Tagak Curley was no longer the only one who thought he knew what was best for his people. Several weeks before he lost his cabinet job, Curley fell into disfavour with many Inuit for not supporting a proposed boundary line to divide the Northwest Territories. Curley rejected the border because the Inuit communities around the Beaufort Sea would have been excluded from Nunavut. Leaving out the Beaufort would defeat Nunavut's purpose of having all Inuit together in one territory, he said. Other northern leaders thought a Nunavut without the Beaufort Sea was better than no Nunavut at all, and turned against Curley. As the founding president of the Inuit Tapirisat of Canada, Tagak Curley "invented Nunavut," said Dennis Patterson, another cabinet minister from the eastern Arctic, but one who supported the division. "He now seems to have changed his mind. Hearing that was like hearing that Rene Levesque had given up on independence for Quebec."

Curley, asserted Patterson during a speech in the legislature, "suggested that aboriginal people will not be able to continue to hunt (on the other side of their respective boundaries) as a result of division. I quote his words: 'You will not be able to hunt here. You are not going to be allowed to trap here'..."

"Cheap shot," Curley blurted.

"I am quoting your words," Patterson said.

"That doesn't mean anything!," shouted a western MLA witnessing with pleasure a breakdown in the unity of eastern Arctic politicians.

"To the people of the West," Patterson continued, "I say let us go our own way, let us pick up and go home..."

"... to Vancouver," Curley interrupted.

"To the people of Nunavut, I say let us go forward with determination and optimism."

"Go home to Vancouver!"

"To Mr. Curley, I say do not be afraid. Do not cling to the status quo."

"I am bloody well not afraid of you, boy."

An impatient Patterson turned to Curley: "Maybe you are getting a little too comfortable in Yellowknife."

Tagak Curley may have been impudent and disrespectful at times, but to him, removal from the executive was rubbing it in. It was a betrayal. In the end, personal grudges, more than the contents of any note, decided Curley's fate.

In his three years as minister of economic development and tourism, Curley was able to overcome political failures with resounding successes. For instance, he laboured in vain to secure jobs for Northerners on a $1.7 billion construction project of a military radar system across the Arctic. But that was overshadowed by the surprise success of the Northwest Territories pavilion at Expo '86 in Vancouver. Curley was the minister responsible for the territorial government's largest and most successful single project ever. It was named the best Canadian pavilion, and placed among the top five pavilions of the entire fair. It featured a country-foods restaurant with Arctic char fillets, reindeer steaks and musk-ox burgers. Thousand-year old ice cubes taken from a glacier in the high Arctic were used to cool beverages. The pavilion introduced nearly two million people to the Northwest Territories and it promised to pay back large dividends in future tourism dollars.

As a cabinet minister in an immense land of many competing cultures and interests, Curley performed an admirable juggling act. Perhaps better than anyone, he maintained the seemingly impossible balance between the North's traditional economy based on hunting and trapping and the new wage-earning economy of the oil and mining industries. Growing up with a foot in each society gave him an advantage over other politicians who knew everything about one world but nothing about the other. Among the Inuit, Curley would wear sealskins and speak Inuktitut. In Yellowknife and other white business centres, he would communicate in English and wear expensive and immaculately custom-tailored suits. He could speak with authority and respect to native groups and chambers of commerce alike. With an uncanny power of persuasion, Curley emerged as a master of back-room politics. He was a confident speaker, although he often appeared nervous. He constantly rubbed his hands together or stroked his curly black hair as he spoke. His speech in English was often rambling and fragmented, but he always tried to look people directly in the eyes, which usually forced him to stand on tiptoe.

By 1987, the government ministers were nearing the end of a four-year term in office and many had become smug. One wanted the department of public works to mow his lawn. Another had his executive assistant pack his suitcases. The ministers started making visits to exotic spots around the globe; Curley visited northern Scandinavia to investigate the economy there. Ordinary members of the legislative assembly would hear nothing about the junkets until after the ministers had returned home.

Ministers appeared indifferent to MLAs' growing frustrations over the government persistently acting in an arbitrary manner. So Tagak Curley was made the scapegoat.

The government as a whole did not take an official position on Curley's fate and ministers were entitled to a free vote. But none of the eight ministers voted to remove Curley. Three, including Dennis Patterson, abstained. Fearful of who might be next, government ministers wanted more than the available two options of either he stays or he goes, or as one minister viewed it: "Hang the person or let him go free." They suggested alternatives, such as referring complaints about a minister's performance to a legislative sub-committee that would recommend an "appropriate punishment." That would have meant that only a handful of legislators would make the important decision of the government's composition. The next step could be leaving it entirely up to the government leader, as in southern Canada. Taking the decision-making powers away from all the MLAs would put the Northwest Territories on the road to party politics. Proponents of the party system often criticized the North's consensus government for an inherent lack of accountability. Curley's removal forced people to recognize that the consensus model did have a mechanism, albeit a brutal one, for ensuring the accountability of government. As a result of the Curley episode, the unique consensus style of governing was solidified in territorial politics. Ironically, Curley's dismissal could go down as the most important of his long list of political achievements.

"This institution has become a true representative of the people of the Northwest Territories, with hard feelings, disagreements, wide gaps of differences and so on," Curley said half-sarcastically after his relegation to the backbench. "But that is a fact of life... I do not hold any grudges against anybody. I have forgiven everybody."

Curley's dismissal meant more than the loss of an effective minister — it was the loss of the only Inuk on the executive. But it opened the door for other Inuit to prove that they too were made of cabinet material. Ludy Pudluk, a twelve-year veteran of the legislative assembly, had always been overlooked for a cabinet post because he had a poor command of English. Curley's departure gave Pudluk the opportunity to dispel the myth that unilingual aboriginal ministers could not deal with the complexities of an English-speaking government. To ensure that there was Inuit representation on the executive council, members of the legislative assembly had little choice but to select Pudluk to replace Curley.

Curley lost the territorial election that autumn to an old political rival who used the impeachment as a campaign issue. Curley himself did not run vigorous election campaigns. Some residents in his riding thought that he believed God would decide his political fate, since he is a deeply religious person. Yet Curley maintained that "God didn't affect my political involvement whatsoever."

Even in public office, Curley had led a very private life. He was a bachelor, but he did not frequent bars and social gatherings, as did so many other northern politicians. With his strong sense of tradition, Curley spent much time on the land, hunting seal and caribou.

A return to a more traditional lifestyle provided a much needed and enjoyable rest after the hectic pace of his political career. He did not want to do anything that smacked of "divide and conquer" tactics, he said, after spending a winter reflecting on his election defeat. "If quality people are running for public office, then I think you shouldn't interfere with a good job that's being carried out."

Yet, if those in office were doing a poor job, then, with the right amount of the old charisma, Tagak Curley could jump back into power as fast as he fell from it. "It's always possible," he admitted.

CECE McCAULEY: THE CHIEF WITH THE FAX

Chief Cece McCauley thought that a bright pink tepee on Parliament Hill would draw a lot of public attention. Instead it attracted "four days of merry-go-round with the bureaucracy."

The Dene chief from Inuvik, N.W.T., wanted to generate publicity for national native leaders who were trying to have the right to aboriginal self-government entrenched in the constitution. They were in Ottawa in March 1987 for a first ministers' constitutional conference. From the tepee, McCauley and others planned to hand out pamphlets and explain the native peoples' goals to the public.

But she arrived in Ottawa and found out there was a new law forbidding squatters on the Parliament grounds. "I threatened to put up my tepee anyway and that I would have all the media there to record the RCMP pushing us around. Then for sure we would get the Canadian people's attention, which was the whole idea."

She reconsidered and decided to take "the diplomatic route." Over the next four days, she visited six federal government departments, the prime minister's office, and even called the prime minister's wife, "but she was out of town." Finally someone suggested that she put the tepee in front of the conference centre where the meetings were being held. The federal government told McCauley that the building belonged to the city of Ottawa and she would have to get its permission. The city told her it belonged to the federal government.

Eventually McCauley received permission from both bureaucracies. But after calling fellow Dene chiefs to arrange a time to set up the tepee, another federal bureaucrat phoned and told McCauley that she had to put the tepee at the back of the conference centre.

"I blew up and said forget the whole damn thing and that I think they're all crazy," McCauley said.

The person at the other end of the phone calmed her and convinced her that the back was a better location because it was where all the media and politicians came in and out of the conference.

"So I brought over my tepee and poles, got a table and chairs and waited and waited. I lost my chiefs. They went to the front of the building and I guess they left when I wasn't there."

She looked for someone else to help put up the tepee and approached a group of native men.

"We're Metis," they told her. "We don't know anything about tepees."

So she asked a group of full-blooded Indians.

"We're from B.C. We don't know anything about tepees."

She phoned the Ottawa office of the Assembly of First Nations, the political organization that represents Canada's status Indians. When she threatened to go to the media and say natives were not ready for self-government, she was told that four men would be sent over "right away." But when only two showed up, McCauley decided that the tepee was not worth the bother.

The next day, a group of Ontario Indians arrived to hold a demonstration outside the convention centre. It started to rain and they asked McCauley if they could set up the tepee for shelter. The publicity gimmick did not work, but it did come in handy for "those poor people," McCauley said. In the end, she sold it to a CBC reporter for $500 and received more orders for the northern-made cotton and polyester tepees.

The story of the pink tepee is typical of Cece McCauley's life as an Indian chief: she is always coming up with outrageous ideas. Everyone thinks she is crazy and will not offer any help. Again and again she fights the bureaucracy and finds a way to salvage something.

Before McCauley came along, the Dene did not have a band in Inuvik. The federal government had built the town in 1953 and encouraged Dene, Inuit and white people to move there from nearby communities. But it would not let the Dene form a band council. The natives "gave up too damn easy," McCauley claimed.

In 1978, McCauley and several others decided to call an election and form a band council, with or without the government's approval. McCauley was elected chief and then set out to get official recognition, which meant $48,000 a year in core funding from the federal government. She had to get letters of support from the other twenty-five chiefs in the Northwest Territories and the Inuvik town council. "The rest was lobby, lobby, lobby. Holy smokes, I've never lobbied so much in my life."

The effort took two years. In 1980, McCauley got the word from Ottawa that Inuvik could have a registered band. She announced the news at a large Dene assembly; everyone hollered and clapped.

McCauley was the Dene's first female chief and for a while most of the other chiefs ignored her. "They didn't associate with me, they looked at me as if I was something different."

Like Dene politics, Dene society is male-dominated. At Dene community feasts, held whenever there is an excuse to celebrate, people gather in the school gymnasium and are served mounds of caribou meat, whitefish, bannock, potatoes, vegetables, Oreo cookies, tea, Kool-aid and whatever else the local hunters shot or the Bay store had in stock that week. In the more isolated and traditional communities, the women — even the oldest one who walks with a cane — and children sit on the floor while the men take their seats at surrounding tables.

Many women still accept that their role is to stand behind their men and be silent. Not McCauley. She thinks that once women get over their shyness, they make the best leaders. "Women chiefs are closer to the people and the day-to-day problems of the family. We're closer to the grassroots."

McCauley likes to ridicule men. In the North, many of them are fond of wearing baseball caps. A meeting of Dene chiefs looks like a baseball dugout. "Some must sleep with their caps on," McCauley once said. "It must be to hold their brains together. Or they're too lazy to wash and comb their hair."

It took about two years before McCauley was accepted by the other chiefs. At a meeting one day, "they came around and talked to me and it was so different, like night and day. I guess they decided I was okay after seeing me at all the meetings where I would pound the table and look at each one of them and say things they never thought of."

An eighty-five-year-old man spoke at a Dene assembly in 1987 and said he thought there should not be any women chiefs — by now there were three. He said they should stay at home and raise children. Then one of the old traditional chiefs who used to ignore McCauley, took the microphone. "We like women chiefs. They ask a lot of good questions."

McCauley is not in the mainstream of Dene political thinking. She likes to stray into controversy to attract attention to a cause. In 1981, when the Dene were claiming aboriginal title to much of the western Northwest Territories and were trying to negotiate a land-claim settlement with Ottawa, the federal government introduced a bill to regulate oil and gas interests in the North. The new law did not recognize the Dene's claim to the land and it referred to most of the territories as "Canada lands." McCauley, wanting to "call their bluff," suggested that the Dene should break away from Canada. This suggestion did not go down well with the other chiefs, who preferred a less drastic course of action. In the end, the chiefs did nothing and the bill was passed by Parliament.

"I bet that if we said then that we've had enough, we're going to sign a trade deal with Russia, shit, then we would have made more waves," McCauley said.

McCauley blames the governments based in Ottawa and Yellowknife for almost everything that is wrong with the North. She has claimed that politicians and bureaucrats "do nothing but sit on their big fat fannies" and "they are here to look after themselves, not the natives." At the same time, she is the first person to greet and wrap her arms around a visiting cabinet minister or senior civil servant. "I sometimes think I embarrass some big wheelers, but I'm like that. I can't change.

"I don't care about class distinctions. I couldn't give a damn if you're white, Indian, Inuit, rich or poor. Too many people put a big shot here and the little guy there. Not me. I get along with everybody."

Officially, McCauley represents the smallest Dene band in the North —fewer than 100 people — but Northerners think of her as a powerful woman. She is influential, she claimed, only because she is an elected official, has a strong personality, and writes a weekly newspaper column that gives her a forum to put her views to readers across the North. Everyone who buys a paper reads the column, even if they hate it.

Her writing is the same as her speech — a rambling mixture of thoughts which jump from one unrelated topic to another, often not paying much attention to accuracy and detail, and sometimes full of contradictions. "I hear some people say I contradict myself. Yes and no," she once told a CBC television reporter. "There's two sides to every story." McCauley has opinions on everything, including the subject of how best to protect northern fur trappers from the animal rights movement: "Just say Greenpeace and everybody knows who they are. Nobody knows this little bunch of Dene. They made a big hit with Bridgette Bardot. We should get a famous person like that on our side. Use Qaddafi if you have to."

She wants whoever in the world is responsible for naming species of animals to change the term for whitefish, which is caught in abundance by northern fishermen. She thinks it would sell better if it had a more exotic name. "Trout and Arctic Char look good on a menu. Maybe whitefish would sell if we called it some Latin name or Eskimo name or Indian name."

In 1983, she suggested that all video games in the North should be run by a women's group that would use the profits to improve sport and recreation centres. Only adults would be allowed to play the games. Video machines would be located in taverns and hotels and "those hazardous arcades that are causing so much hardship to families with children would be eliminated."

So children could receive a better education, McCauley has suggested that classes run from one o'clock until the evening. "You know why there's poor attendance at school?" she asked. "It's because of Betamax. Parents are up all night playing poker or drinking and the kids watch TV. Even in good families, kids don't go to bed early. Native people are too soft. You can shout down Main Street, but you can't pound it into their heads that the kids have to go to school at nine. So the thing to do is start at one, then everyone can still stay up all night and get up at noon. It should be tried as a pilot project.

"Nobody's taking me seriously so I'm threatening to start my own school and try it," she added.

"When I stick up for natives," she said, many white people get upset with her. But she remains unrepentant. "I like to say, look, read the Indian history — see what you did to us."

"The Canadian and American people know that their natives own this land, that we belong here. They know we've got that over their heads, that this was our land and we let them in as friends. I think that's why they treasure their natives in a way. The Americans aren't as prejudiced with natives as they are with Negroes. I think we're even better off than the Jews.

"The people who are prejudiced are assholes anyway," she continued. "You know who the hell they are, so you don't pay any attention to them. But if they are in government and they treat my people badly, I'm going to make sure they get out or they apologize."

McCauley saw racism for the first time during World War II, shortly after the atomic bomb was dropped on Hiroshima. The uranium for the bomb was mined at Port Radium, on the shores of Great Bear Lake, near the trapline where McCauley grew up.

An airplane load of newspaper reporters and photographers from around the world arrived one day and they wanted to take pictures of local Indian girls holding some uranium. McCauley appeared in *Maclean's* magazine and her niece was in *Time*. "That made all the white women there jealous."

For several years during the war, the Great Bear Lake and Norman Wells area was taken over by hundreds of American servicemen who worked to extract local uranium and oil for the war effort. "We all fell in love with them and big affairs started all along the Mackenzie," recalled McCauley, who was in her early twenties at the time.

McCauley was working for the Americans as a cook when a doctor asked her to marry him. "I couldn't believe it. A doctor to us was like a god. I was too green to be a doctor's wife." Instead, Cece married a white fur trader and trapper named Jim McCauley. She had had five years of schooling at a Catholic convent, but her husband "was my real teacher. He taught me how to read and how to speak properly. He read every book on earth, I think. He would carry Shakespeare along on the trapline."

McCauley now reads every "good" book and magazine on the shelf. "I don't mean magazines like *Love Story*. I buy the ones which I'll learn something from. All the town people think I'm crazy when I buy the *Financial Post*. If they only knew what's in there."

Her husband was well read, but he also drank a lot. They had two sons before they divorced, and he later died. "I was petrified of alcohol. I grew up very sheltered. I didn't even swear then. I didn't touch alcohol until I was thirty-seven, after I came to Inuvik, and I still have never smoked."

McCauley moved to Inuvik in 1958 to work at a general store for a friend. Then she started her controversial political career.

McCauley runs a modern band office. It was one of the first Dene bands to use computers and by 1988 it was the only one with a FAX machine. While many of the 12,500 Dene live a traditional lifestyle of hunting and trapping and fishing, the Dene of Inuvik live in a modern town that is the base for oil company activities in the Beaufort Sea and Mackenzie River delta. McCauley wanted to get the band involved in business ventures and it seemed only natural to join the oil rush. Perhaps, she thought, the band could buy a drilling rig and receive contract work with one of the multinational oil corporations. She was constantly travelling to Ottawa to lobby for a government loan. Her band councillors became angry because the chief, who never seemed to be in Inuvik, did not consult them about her plans. They phoned her in Ottawa one Friday in 1983 and asked for her resignation. She caught the first plane back to Inuvik and the councillors agreed to meet with her on the Monday. McCauley then flew back half way up the Mackenzie River to Norman Wells for the weekend and made an eleventh hour pitch to Imperial Oil to support her oil deal. While there, a CBC radio reporter interviewed her about her plans. The band councillors in Inuvik heard the report, thought the idea was foolish, and decided to throw her out of office.

"Some big hit I made on the radio," McCauley said. "But I didn't care. If my band wanted to struggle on a shoe string, that's their business. But as chief, I wanted my people to be self-sufficient, so I went and looked for oil." She returned to Inuvik and praised her councillors "because I think they did what they thought was right." After listening to her, they decided to give her another chance.

A year later, McCauley was still chasing her oil deal and she also had a scheme to open a chain of grocery stores in the western Arctic. With a partner, the band opened a store in the small Beaufort coastal community of Paulatuk. Then McCauley answered a tender call to supply food to the Imperial Oil camp at Norman Wells. "We were second. They gave it to the lowest bidder, who was too low. They had to add on more money to what he bid to help him survive. We had a better deal. They should have given it to us."

By this time the band was over $150,000 in debt with nothing to show for it and the councillors had had enough. They asked McCauley to resign. She agreed, but the band elections were soon approaching and she warned them that she would again run for the position of chief.

Although the election was set for June 29, 1984, the band postponed it for a month when McCauley was the only person to file nomination papers. Two more people were recruited, but McCauley was re-elected nevertheless. She now agreed not to pursue any more outlandish business ventures without first consulting her band councillors.

The councillors gave McCauley the nod to go after a thirty-two-unit abandoned apartment building in Inuvik that was owned by the federal government. McCauley wanted it turned over to the band, which would renovate and lease it. The Department of Indian Affairs and Northern Development agreed to the plan, but the building belonged to the Department of Public Works. Indian Affairs had to find a building of equal value and trade it for the Inuvik apartment. About a year later, a structure in La Pas, Manitoba was given to Public Works and the Inuvik band received its apartment.

McCauley went to the bank for a loan for the renovations, but was told she could not borrow any money because, although the band owned the apartment, it did not own the land. So she went back to Indian Affairs and asked for the land. That took another year. In the meantime, the Conservatives came to power and the federal purse strings suddenly tightened. The Treasury Board told Indian Affairs that the land could not be given away — it was worth $400,000. Three years later, it was appraised again and it was worth half as much. Indian Affairs agreed to pay $200,000 to the Treasury Board and, in 1988, the land was finally turned over to the Inuvik band.

By then the band's financial condition had improved. McCauley planned to edge her band into other business enterprises, but there would be no gambles. In 1986, she opened her own restaurant at the Inuvik airport. Whitefish was on the menu, of course, but she was still hoping to give it an exotic name. By then several more women had become Dene chiefs and one community, Fort Smith, had voted in an all-female band council.

Today, life for McCauley is so good that "when I wake up each morning I feel like doing a jig. I can't believe I'm doing half the things I'm doing. Sometimes I think I'm not real." Many people would agree.

STEPHEN KAKFWI: A GOOD TIME TO SETTLE A LAND CLAIM

Stephen Kakfwi had heard enough rhetoric. The time had come to settle the Dene claim to land in the western part of the Northwest Territories.

For almost a decade, negotiations with Ottawa had been nothing more than on-again, off-again bouts of verbal combat. Dene leaders went into a meeting and said that they were entitled to 450,000 square miles — the entire Mackenzie River Valley — and all the oil under the ground. Federal negotiators said that the Dene should be thankful for whatever land the government turned over and they should not even consider getting a drop of the oil.

Both sides took a more realistic approach after 1983, when Kakfwi was elected president of the Dene Nation, the political organization that represents the Northwest Territories' 12,500 Indians.

"For the number of people we have, we're not going to get all the land. I think we're obliged to use our judgement to realize that," Kakfwi said.

Convincing Ottawa to take the Dene seriously and bargain in good faith was his immediate task. But some politicians could never be persuaded. In 1985, Kakfwi walked out of a meeting in Yellowknife with Suzanne Blais-Grenier, who was then the federal environment minister, because she refused to make a plan to create northern wildlife conservation areas conditional on a land-claim settlement.

"She just appeared so indifferent and insolent, so I left. I couldn't be bothered with it," Kakfwi said. "But I didn't lose my temper. I know the media perception at the time was that I had a big fight with the minister. I never denied it because I thought, well, let her explain." Blais-Grenier played down the incident and said that Kakfwi was annoyed because he had not received an early notice of the meeting. She was dropped from the federal Cabinet about a week later because she was considered an ineffective minister. Kakfwi thought the demotion was "great."

The minister of Indian affairs and northern development was the cabinet member who Kakfwi had to confront most often. But when Saskatchewan farmer William McKnight, the fourth Indian Affairs minister during his first three years as Dene Nation president, showed little interest in travelling north after his appointment to the portfolio in 1986, Kakfwi did not seem to care. "I've stopped getting excited about meeting these people," he said at the time.

Every new minister had his own style. "Some of them don't keep commitments, some of them don't make commitments, and some of them don't know what they're talking about."

While ministers rotated, the bureaucrats kept a firm grasp on the activities of the department. So Kakfwi worked to "soften them up and treat them well and get them on side." That usually helped when it came time for the minister to make a decision. But Indian Affairs is a relatively minor portfolio and the Department of Justice has the final say in any political negotiations. "Justice was always there staring over the shoulders of all these ministers," Kakfwi said. "Justice was the law, so to speak, on what was and what wasn't negotiable and acceptable."

But everything eventually fit together. In 1987 Kakfwi stepped down as president of the Dene Nation and was elected to the Northwest Territories legislature, subsequently becoming minister of education and of aboriginal rights and constitutional development. The following year negotiators reached an agreement-in-principle on a land-claim settlement that would make the Dene and Metis the largest landholders, except for governments, in North America. They would receive 70,000 square miles of land, $500 million, a share of resource revenues throughout the Mackenzie Valley, and representation on land, resource and wildlife management boards. The agreement was presented at the Dene national assembly — an annual gathering where hundreds of delegates from the Northwest Territories' twenty-six Dene communities, during a week marked by outdoor camping, feasts and drum dances, set Dene Nation policies and elect its executive. In 1988, they had to decide whether to accept or reject the proposed land-claim agreement. The Dene eventually signed, but many delegates complained that 70,000 square miles was not enough land and they should hold out for more. Some were critical that the agreement made no mention of aboriginal self-government, but the omission was not surprising. The Dene Nation had decided in 1982 not to negotiate for self-government in its land-claim. Instead, it would seek guaranteed representation for the Dene in the territorial government through its participation in the Western Constitutional Forum, which was charged with constitutional development for the western part of the Northwest Territories.

Kakfwi believed the Dene should continue to negotiate its political rights within the governmental system rather than set up separate reserves on which the Dene could exercise self-government. Furthermore, to include self-government in the land-claim settlement now would only prolong negotiations for many more years, he said. "We can't afford to wait. We have no protection now and we will have even less protection in five years... The Dene Nation isn't going to stop the mining. It isn't going to stop the oil exploration. It hasn't done it in the past, it won't do it in the future."

Although Kakfwi was no longer president of the Dene Nation, the agreement stemmed from negotiations he had directed and he promoted it more than any other Dene leader. If the Dene did not accept the land-claim agreement, "then you will need a whole new bunch of leaders to head up negotiations," Kakfwi told the delegates. "Some of us have worked for many years and we're not interested in going through the whole thing again."

After Kakfwi spoke, another former president of the Dene Nation took the microphone. Georges Erasmus told delegates that the deal was "garbage." In a strong and emotional speech, with a storm brewing and winds howling around him, he said that the agreement is what the government "thinks it can get away with" and suggested the Dene return to the bargaining table.

"If those people around us are tired because they have been doing this for fifteen years, then maybe they should leave," he said in obvious reference to Kakfwi. "If there are some leaders among us who feel they are not up to the challenge of defending this land and these people, and mainly the people who are not born yet, then maybe their contributions are over. Maybe they have given us their best... I haven't given up."

The clash between the Dene's two most influential leaders marked a public return to an old political rivalry that dated back to their early years in the aboriginal rights movement.

In 1974, Kakfwi quit his job as an adult educator in Hay River, Northwest Territories, because he was not given a promotion or pay raise, while an American teacher whom Kakfwi had trained the previous year received both. Kakfwi was on his way home to Fort Good Hope, a small community on the shores of the Mackenzie River, when he stopped in Yellowknife for a visit. He passed by the head office of the Dene Nation (which was then called the Indian Brotherhood of the Northwest Territories), where Georges Erasmus was employed as the director of a programme to organize politically the Dene communities. Erasmus hired Kakfwi as a fieldworker in Fort Good Hope. But two weeks later, Erasmus phoned to say that he did not realize Kakfwi was a non-status Indian and therefore could not work for the Indian Brotherhood. "I didn't care at the time, but I never forgot it," Kakfwi said.

Kakfwi is a full-blooded Dene, but he lost his Indian status in 1957, when he was seven years old. His grandfather signed away the family's rights covered by Treaty 11, which the Dene of the Mackenzie Valley signed with the federal government in 1921, because he thought the collective approach of the treaty interfered with the way he wanted to run his fur-trading business and his desire to own private property. Stephen Kakfwi regained his status in 1988, at the age of thirty-seven, as a political safeguard against Dene critics who questioned his ability to discuss the old Indian treaties in terms of the present land-claim negotiations. (While Ottawa wanted a land-claim to replace treaty rights, the Dene wanted to keep these rights — which include free eye glasses, health and dental care, and an annual payment of five dollars — as part of any land-claim settlement.)

Since the Indian Brotherhood did not want him in 1974, Kakfwi went to work for the Metis Association of the Northwest Territories. Until 1977, he organized submissions and testimonies of groups and individuals in Fort Good Hope and other communities to be presented to the Mackenzie Valley Pipeline Inquiry. After a three-year inquiry, Justice Thomas Berger recommended a ten-year moratorium on the construction of a pipeline to allow time for the settlement of land-claims.

In 1976, Erasmus was elected president of the Indian Brotherhood. He wanted the Dene and Metis united in one organization, since the federal government would only negotiate one land-claim settlement for the Mackenzie Valley. The Metis rejected the idea because they saw themselves as a distinct culture of Dene and white descent. The Indian Brotherhood opened its membership to include Metis and non-status Dene anyway, which angered the Metis leaders. But Kakfwi took advantage of the move and he was again hired by Erasmus.

This time, Kakfwi lasted four years before there was a dispute. As an assistant to the president, Kakfwi thought Erasmus was losing touch with the communities and that he wielded too much control in the Yellowknife head office. Erasmus was in charge of everything — researching and negotiating the claim, the day-to-day office administration, and dealing with politicians on other matters, such as the desperate need for housing and education in Indian communities. Kakfwi thought that the president should just behave like a politician, while a separate chief negotiator handled the land-claim talks and an executive director took care of the office. He and other staff members developed a strategy for re-organization, but, Kakfwi said, Erasmus would not even consider it.

To register his concerns to the Dene public, Kakfwi announced four days before the 1980 Dene national assembly that he was challenging Erasmus for the presidency. "It's important to get the work done, but how we do the work is equally or more important," Kakfwi told the delegates. "It makes a hell of a lot of difference when the president is sitting beside the chief when he is deciding issues."

Delegates thought it would not be wise to change leaders when a land-claim settlement appeared to be near, and Erasmus won the election 158 votes to twenty-nine.

The election contest created a lasting bitterness between the two men. It was as much a clash of personalities as philosophies; Erasmus is the passionate idealist while Kakfwi is a cool pragmatist. The latter's preference for the concrete over the theoretical was revealed at a human rights conference in 1986, where a debate about collective versus individual rights left Kakfwi somewhat perplexed. When asked to speak, he told the experts: "I'm not a philosopher, so I may confuse you a little. I'm not a lawyer either, so you may find me a little boring. And I'm not a theologian either, so I won't be dragging Him into it... I just think that when you're a majority it's easy to sit back and say everyone should be treated the same, but the aboriginal people want to be recognized as a collective."

After a brief "self-imposed exile" in Quebec City to be with his future wife, Marie Wilson, a CBC radio reporter who had worked in Yellowknife, Kakfwi returned to Fort Good Hope in 1981 and worked on economic development projects for the local Dene band. "After all the rhetoric we (Dene leaders) were preaching in the seventies about traditional lifestyle, self-determination and community development, we all felt we had to get our feet wet — we had to go do it. All of us moved back to the communities. Just about all of us — people like Georges never did."

In 1983, after seven years as Dene Nation president, Erasmus went on to Ottawa to become the chief of the Assembly of First Nations, the national organization representing status Indians, and turned his attention to entrenching aboriginal rights in the Canadian constitution. A Dene land-claim settlement was still a long way off, and Erasmus's relationship with Metis leaders had not improved. An exasperated federal government stopped negotiations until the two groups started to work together.

When Erasmus stepped down, Kakfwi was a house husband in Yellowknife while his wife worked at the CBC. He ran for president again and this time won with sixty-two percent of the votes. One of the candidates he defeated, a former vice-president of the Dene Nation, was considered philosophically identical to Erasmus. The day after Kakfwi's election victory, Erasmus could not be found anywhere in Fort Resolution, the host community of the assembly that year. He had chartered an airplane and left at five in the morning.

The presidential transition was not smooth. Erasmus's people did not turn over their research and previous work on the land-claim, and Kakfwi did not ask for their services. Kakfwi implemented the "collective team approach" that he proposed in 1980. And he declared that the strained relationship with the Metis was "no longer a problem."

Why?

"I don't know," Kakfwi said. "Because I'm a good guy I guess."

More likely, it was because he accepted the theory that the Dene and Metis were indeed distinct cultural groups, even though they shared the same land. He and a new slate of Metis leaders decided to settle the claim first and worry later about how they would split the property, money and powers. To negotiate their joint claim, the Dene and Metis agreed to set up a secretariat with one chief negotiator who would answer to the leadership of both groups.

With the Metis satisfied and the land-claim talks again underway, Kakfwi was let loose to pursue other matters of importance to the Dene. Increasingly concerned about native hunting and trapping rights, he helped organize Indigenous Survival International, a world-wide aboriginal lobby to counter the growing animal rights movement. And after reading a newspaper article about Pope John Paul's request to meet the native people of Canada, Kakfwi convinced national aboriginal groups and Canadian bishops to let the Dene, most of whom claim to be Roman Catholic, host and organize a papal visit. He travelled to the Vatican twice for an audience with the Pope, and it was a political coup when he guided the Pope around the community of Fort Simpson in September 1987.

While Kakfwi was the president of the Dene Nation every aspect of northern political life was dominated by a desire on the part of the Inuit to divide the Northwest Territories, and create a new territory in the Eastern Arctic. It was an issue the Dene could not avoid and, in 1985, Kakfwi became chairman of the Western Constitutional Forum, which was negotiating a boundary line with an eastern counterpart. However, splitting up land was not easy and the usually bitter talks damaged the already weak bonds between West and East, and Dene and Inuit. The day before Kakfwi and the president of the Metis Association were to fly to an Arctic community to speak to a conference of Inuit leaders, the chairman of the Eastern Forum called to say that they were no longer invited. "He was afraid we would intimidate delegates from speaking openly and honestly," Kakfwi said. He went anyway.

At the conference, the Inuit were thinking of asking the federal government to draw the border line. "The people of the Northwest Territories have to decide this issue," Kakfwi told the Inuit. "We don't want Ottawa to make any more decisions for us."

Many Dene leaders did not think that Ottawa would give the West a fair deal because officials in the Department of Indian Affairs and Northern Development are perceived to be more sympathetic to Inuit, whose land and culture are often romanticized by southern Canadians. During one meeting in Ottawa, a bureaucrat tried to assure Kakfwi that no such favouritism existed. Kakfwi took note of the Inuit drawings and soapstone carvings in the office and asked him, if he held no bias, then "where's all your Indian art?"

Attempts to embarrass or shame people into action is a political trick that Kakfwi exercised often. He boycotted Expo '86 in Vancouver in support of the Haida Indians on the west coast of British Columbia. Since the provincial government refused to negotiate a land-claim settlement with the Haida, "I'm not going to be a tourist spending money down there," he said at the time.

Kakfwi's Expo protest caused some discomfort for officials in the Government of the Northwest Territories, which had sunk $9 million into a pavilion that would sell native arts and crafts, serve country foods and feature northern cultural performers. There was too much at stake to support a boycott. "If Steve Kakfwi doesn't go, it's not going to impact us that much," said Nick Sibbeston, then Northwest Territories government leader.

"I don't know if our priorities are the same," Kakfwi later said of Sibbeston, who had offered to pay the City of Yellowknife to rename its streets with aboriginal words.

"That for me is not a priority," said Kakfwi, who thought money could be put to more practical uses, such as hiring back Dene language translators who had been laid off because of federal cutbacks. "I guess I have problems with the way government works the same as everyone else."

Kakfwi knocked the Northwest Territories government harder than other groups because he expected support "from a government that is supposed to be sympathetic to native people." He even criticized it for giving preference to aboriginal people when awarding contracts and jobs because "it is not doing anything to enhance the image of native people in the business community."

And he had been attacking the education system ever since he quit his teaching job in Hay River. "When I look at the money spent on education during the last fifteen years and see how many of our people are educated — it's a laugh," he said in 1983, minutes after he was elected Dene Nation president.

Kakfwi's election to the legislature in 1987, and his subsequent appointment as minister of education and of aboriginal rights and constitutional development, gave him the opportunity to act on his complaints about the government. His new position also meant that he could continue to be a force in the ongoing land-claim negotiations.

The Dene and federal government were now working to turn their land-claim agreement-in-principle into a final agreement. Kakfwi was not sure if the new Dene leaders had enough experience to meet the challenge. "I'd like to say that I have full confidence in the Dene Nation executive and the chiefs, but I don't. I think they will need a lot of help from people like both myself and Georges Erasmus, people with success under their belts.

"One way or another, I'm going to play a role."

LYNDA SORENSEN: SHEDDING A REDNECK IMAGE

For a long time Lynda Sorensen was notorious for defending the rights of white people and trying to bring southern-style politics into the North. Then one day she started to work quietly for the Dene.

It should have been big news in 1985, but at the time, Sorensen, a former outspoken member of the Northwest Territories legislative assembly, was not seeking publicity.

"I didn't want a big write-up in the press about Lynda Sorensen going to work for the Dene Nation. There was a little blurb, but I remained very low key. That was very difficult for me, having had a very high profile for the previous ten years."

Politics in the Northwest Territories is often dominated by conflicts between natives and whites, rural and urban, and East and West (which is not surprising considering the territory comprises one-third of Canada's total land mass). As a white MLA from the city of Yellowknife from 1979 to 1983, Sorensen always seemed to be in the thick of every battle.

For her, the legislature was often a lonely place. She was the only MLA to protest plans for a territorial-wide plebiscite in 1982 to see if people wanted to divide the Northwest Territories into two separate territories. The Inuit passionately wanted to create a new territory in the Eastern Arctic to be called Nunavut, which would evolve into an Inuit homeland. Sorensen, who thought Northerners should build unity rather than barriers, grilled the Inuit over the topic.

"Any support from myself and my constituents for Nunavut will not be blind support," she said in 1980. "It must be earned, not given because of sympathy or because some might think native people have been done an injustice in the past."

At about the same time, Sorensen also fought to keep available to white students the Northwest Territories government's generous postsecondary student loans and grants. Native MLAs claimed that very few aboriginal people were benefitting from them and the money would be better spent on the lower grades so native children could be given a chance to go to university.

"It was a very racist debate and it really hurt to be involved in something like that," she recalled eight years later. "It also aroused the worst in Yellowknife and the communities around Great Slave Lake because that's where the majority of non-natives live and our children were witness to that. I hated that whole thing."

In June 1980, many rural MLAs — native and white — were also against the idea of spending $25 million to build a new modern hospital in Yellowknife. The new hospital was to be built in Sorensen's constituency, which is a large suburb populated predominantly by white civil servants and businessmen. In contrast to most of the poor rural villages in the North, there has been nothing but economic growth in Yellowknife since it was made the territorial capital in 1967. To have a modern hospital in the city, more doctors and medical specialists would have to be hired.

"It seems to me everybody focuses on how to get more stuff into Yellowknife," said Nellie Cournoyea, an MLA representing several small communities around the Beaufort Sea, during a debate in the legislature. "What is in Yellowknife that is going to attract more doctors and better doctors? Are you saying that Yellowknife is so attractive and has so much to offer..."

"Yes," interrupted Sorensen.

"I am wondering really what is going on behind the scenes," Cournoyea continued. "I am wondering if possibly there is a little scheme going on to discourage doctors from going farther than Yellowknife."

"Shame, shame!" Sorensen shouted.

Sorensen and another Yellowknife MLA decided that they would try to keep the debate going until they won. Legislators eventually agreed that a large, modern hospital in the capital city would benefit all Northerners because patients would not have to be treated as far away as Edmonton. During the debate, Sorensen pointed to an Inuit MLA who had suffered a stroke years earlier, and said: "The very fact that he came to Yellowknife saved his life because had he been on the plane going to Edmonton, he may not have survived that long."

Sorensen knew such details because she had been the head nurse at the Yellowknife hospital. She worked there after following her journalist husband north from Alberta in 1970. Art Sorensen opened the northern bureau for the *Edmonton Journal*.

Lynda Sorensen quit her nursing career in 1973 to have her second child. While at home with the baby, she did volunteer work for the Consumer's Association of Canada. That led to the full-time job of opening and running a Yellowknife office for the association. She became a consumer advocate, commenting publicly on everything from the price of food to the delivery of government services.

Being in the public eye prompted her to run successfully for the legislature in 1979, at the age of thirty-two. At the same time, she became active in the federal Liberal Party as president of the Western Arctic riding association. "I was in a position to do something, to change things through political activity. I felt I had an obligation not to just complain all the time, and not to just continue making observations."

She chose the Liberals because she agreed with their ideology and because they were in power at the time. Northern politicians are a pragmatic lot when it comes to party politics. Many MLAs were card-carrying members of the Liberal Party during the days of Pierre Trudeau. Others joined the Tories when Brian Mulroney came to power. It helped to have connections at the federal level. At the territorial level, politicians are elected as independents without party tags; there is no governing party, no opposition, no third party.

Until 1947, only Southerners were appointed to the territorial council (forerunner to the legislative assembly). The first elected member in the hybrid council of elected and appointed members won a seat in 1951. No native person was appointed until 1965 and no native person was elected until 1967. The assembly was not fully elected until 1975, but even then the federally appointed commissioner still held most of the power. Elected representatives did not make all the territorial government's decisions until 1986, when the government leader took over the commissioner's remaining responsibilities of hiring government personnel and chairing cabinet meetings.

The goal of pursuing the North's self-interests and fighting Ottawa for more constitutional responsibilities was the idea behind the creation of the Northern Party in the spring of 1983. Sorensen announced her intention to run in that fall's territorial election as a Northern Party candidate and a half-dozen others were expected to follow. It looked as though party politics was on its way, but the Northern Party never made it to the campaign trail.

The party was an unusual coalition of federal Liberals and Conservatives. Everything seemed to run smoothly as long as both parties were even in the national polls. But when the Tories' fortunes went up, they figured they could do it on their own and pulled out of the Northern Party.

To explain their decision, the Conservatives said they were not able to figure out what the Northern Party was all about. "Theoretically, if the Northern Party had run candidates, all twenty-four seats would have been filled by them because they had such a great platform," said Bruce McLaughlin, a territorial MLA who sat on the Conservative Party's national executive. "And then what would have happened? Everyone would have belonged to the same party and it would have been a consensus government."

With the Conservatives out of the picture, the Liberals went as well. The Northern Party did not want to be seen as "a bunch of disaffected Liberals," Sorensen said.

Afterwards, there was the occasional rumbling from a few MLAs with half-hearted desires to develop politics along the established party lines. But most legislators enjoyed their independence from party discipline and their freedom to set their own goals. Federal Liberals, such as Sorensen and Nellie Cournoyea, continued to debate each other as always and government by consensus remained the accepted model for the Northwest Territories legislature.

"In my heart, I still feel strongly about the Northern Party concept," Sorensen said in the aftermath of the party's collapse. She now thought the party could field federal candidates in the territories and northern parts of the provinces. "There are tremendous possibilities for a party in the North that could never win a national election because we would never have the seats, but in making a statement in the way the NDP have made a statement. The NDP started in Saskatchewan with a bunch of farmers as a base — that's how parties start.

"But if you're going to be a leader in any movement, you've got to have followers," she conceded.

With the Northern Party going nowhere, Sorensen devoted her political attention to the Liberals. She became the president of the Liberal women's commission and a member of the party's inner management committee, she co-chaired a national policy convention, and she has been a faithful supporter of party leader John Turner.

In 1984, she resigned her seat in the legislature to run for the Liberals in the federal election. "I had always been a supporter of women running, so it was something I couldn't turn my back on," she said. "We women complain a lot about not being there, so when it's your time and you don't run, how can you ever ask why aren't there any women in power?"

Sorensen finished third. Financially broke as a result of the campaign, she had to find a job. She approached Stephen Kakfwi, the president of the Dene Nation. "I was quite nervous about it because I did have a reputation of being somewhat of a redneck from my days in the legislature. But I always felt bad in the legislature when I appeared to be taking a role that proved to be a threat to the aboriginal people. But I felt the questions had to be asked because if they couldn't answer them, then they weren't doing their cause any good."

Sorensen told Kakfwi that she would settle for a low wage because she really wanted to work for the Dene. "I wasn't particularly interested in going to work for the government as a bureaucrat because I really am a political animal."

Kakfwi thought about it for a few days before telling Sorensen that she was "too hot to handle."

Sorensen said she understood, "but the next time we talk, it'll cost you more."

She worked as a bureaucrat for eight months until Kakfwi phoned with a job offer. "Okay, but it'll cost you more," she said.

Kakfwi took a lot of heat from the Dene chiefs when he hired Sorensen as an "executive consultant." And on the streets of Yellowknife, cynics thought Sorensen was trying to build a profile for herself in the Dene communities to help in her next bid for a federal seat. But Sorensen just kept quiet and did her job, writing position papers and advising Dene leaders on government issues.

She had to "hold my nose" a couple of times. Although Sorensen holds the Liberal Party's position that Canada should be friendly with the United States and help it defend the continent, she once wrote a brief to Parliament's standing committee on national defence stating the Dene Nation's position that Canada should be a neutral and nuclear-free country. "It was a very good paper," she said. "The NDP were falling all over themselves commending us and trying to get a copy."

While she was working for them in 1987, the Dene chiefs also came out in support of a proposal to divide the Northwest Territories. Sorensen still personally believed division was not in the North's best interests, "but I'm not the raving lunatic that I was when we were debating it in the legislature."

Sorensen did not run for a seat in the legislature again partially because "I had left territorial politics and now I see myself more on the national level." But she did not consider another run at a federal Liberal nomination either. "Somehow the further I get from being a politician, the nicer it is. It is wonderful to be at home most evenings with my family and lead a normal life after being out all the time and travelling."

When Kakfwi was made the minister of education in the territorial government in 1987, he hired Sorensen as his executive assistant.

"What can be perceived by some as coming down in stature is not a big problem for me," she said. "I never felt that I was all that important as an ordinary MLA anyway."

But Sorensen could not escape entirely from the trappings of politics. Working with a politician, she said, was the next best thing to being one.

PETER ITTINUAR: TO OTTAWA AND BACK

For a brief sweet moment, Peter Ittinuar was the greatest hope for Canada's native people.

He was the most intelligent, educated, articulate and handsome Inuk any southern Canadian had ever seen. He studied political science at Carleton University and taught Inuktitut to inquisitive white students at the University of Ottawa before moving on to a career in politics. Nobody imagined he would slide into a listless life with no job, a broken family and few friends.

In 1979, at the age of twenty-nine, Ittinuar, running as an NDP candidate, was the first Inuit to be elected to the House of Commons. His constituents were almost all Inuit living in the new eastern Arctic riding of Nunatsiaq, which encompasses over two million square kilometers — everything above the treeline. He enjoyed the life of a member of Parliament: the instant recognition, the generous salary, the social parties, and he could take a case of Molson Canadian to his office in the Confederation block of the century-old Parliament buildings if a boyhood friend from the North dropped in for a visit.

Maybe he did not respect the institution, but he did take his job seriously. On the NDP benches, Ittinuar helped convince the governing Liberals to recognize aboriginal rights in the Constitution. With persistent lobbying, he persuaded the government to grant the wish of most Inuit and agree to create a new territory in the eastern Arctic to be called Nunavut, which means "our land" in Inuktitut.

Prime Minister Pierre Trudeau originally opposed the idea of splitting the North because it appeared to him to be a proposal for another Quebec — a division based on ethnic lines with the Inuit in one territory and the Dene and whites in another. He apparently changed his mind at a 1982 Liberal Party policy convention when John Munro, then the minister of Indian affairs and northern development, assured Trudeau that white people would not be excluded from Nunavut. Munro added that the Inuit had supported the federal government in the Quebec referendum on sovereignty association. "Almost every single Canadian of Inuit descent fought long and hard at your side to defeat Rene Levesque," Munro told Trudeau.

Admitting he had been "absolutely spellbound" by the Inuit support, Trudeau responded that he could support territorial division "with the kind of assurances you say are forthcoming."

Peter Ittinuar listened to the exchange and remarked that it seemed cabinet approval of division hinged on whether the Inuit remained "good Liberals."

When support for the principle of dividing the Northwest Territories was formally announced two weeks later, Ittinuar himself became a good Liberal, crossing the floor from the New Democrat benches to show his appreciation to the government.

Party tags mean little to people in the Arctic, where political candidates are known personally and elections are more or less popularity contests. And since parties were insignificant to his constituents, Ittinuar abandoned the NDP without hesitation. He was quick to make friends in the Liberal Party. He had an independent streak that fit in well with the Trudeau mold, and his lifestyle didn't hurt either. Ittinuar is tall with jet black hair and complementary moustache, and well dressed by southern standards. Only the hair colour fit the Inuit stereotype. Always flamboyant, he was known to House of Commons security guards as the MP who buzzed around Parliament Hill on a motorcycle with the word "Eskimo" painted on his helmet.

Ittinuar counted Pierre Trudeau as one of his friends. He guided the prime minister and his three sons on an Arctic tour and summer camping trip in 1983. There were constant rumours of a new junior cabinet portfolio — a minister of state for aboriginal rights — in the works for Ittinuar. However, his ministerial aspirations were halted by Trudeau's resignation and the subsequent federal election in 1984. Ittinuar had to return North to fight another campaign. When he arrived home, he found that he was unwanted. The affection that southern Liberals afforded him was not shared by northern Liberals, who were mostly old political enemies and rivals. The president of the Nunatsiaq Liberal Association, Tagak Curley, was the man Ittinuar had defeated as a New Democrat in 1979.

Without the support of the party association's executive, Ittinuar did not even bother to seek the Liberal nomination. Instead, he ran as an independent. He had no campaign money to canvass the largest and most remote electoral district in Canada, and he finished a humiliating last: just 668 of the 9,882 electors voted for him.

"It's a hard job baby, let somebody else do it for a while," he said as he watched the election results come in.

As if this was not demoralizing enough, Ittinuar also had legal problems. His first brush with the law had taken place shortly after his election to Parliament, when he weathered a conviction and a $200 fine for possession of a small amount of cocaine. NDP Leader Ed Broadbent publicly supported and stood by his young MP at that troubled time, a gesture for which Ittinuar remained forever grateful. A few years later, while campaigning in the 1984 election, Ittinuar was again involved in lengthy and expensive legal proceedings back in Ottawa. He was charged with theft, breach of trust and using a forged document to obtain $5,200 in federal expenses for a constituency visit he never made. The first two charges were dropped for a lack of evidence and he eventually was acquitted on the final charge by a jury in December 1985.

During the days of the trial, Ittinuar married Susan Munro against the wishes of her father, John Munro, the former minister of Indian affairs and northern development. John Munro and Ittinuar had had a falling out the previous year, when Munro was taking a run at the Liberal leadership to succeed Trudeau. The day before the leadership convention, Ittinuar withdrew his support for Munro and voted for Jean Chretien. Every other Liberal delegate from the eastern Arctic stuck with Munro until the end. Ittinuar claimed that Munro never had a chance of winning and it was more important to rally support behind Chretien in order to defeat John Turner, who the Inuit considered an unknown. Munro refused to attend his daughter's wedding, and Ittinuar's friend and mentor became the despised father-in-law.

With no jobs, no money, and a new-born daughter, the couple moved to Rankin Inlet, Ittinuar's home community on the west coast of Hudson Bay. Crude jokes about "how long she will last" circulated around town when Peter brought Susan "home." Ittinuar himself found it difficult to adjust to the change of life in a small northern town. "I've been back a year and I've had a chance to observe some things," he said in an interview over a bottle of Scotch in a Rankin Inlet hotel room in the spring of 1986. "The North is not a happy situation."

While he was away, Rankin Inlet had grown into a regional government administration centre of over 1,000 people, many of whom were white civil servants from the South. The town had become a community of "social cliques based on race," Ittinuar said. "I am amazed at the depth of racism and ignorance of both non-native and Inuit people. And it has been years since these people have been living together."

The two racial groups in Rankin Inlet rarely interact, either socially or in the work place. Being a racially mixed family, the Ittinuars found that they were not accepted by either society. Neither Ittinuar nor his wife were able to find jobs and within months the marriage met an ugly end. After a domestic dispute in November 1985, Ittinuar was charged with two counts of beating Susan and one of assaulting an RCMP officer who was trying to intervene. Ittinuar pleaded guilty and was fined $850. Susan took their daughter and returned to Ottawa, leaving behind forever the nightmare of Rankin Inlet.

After the breakup of his marriage, the former member of Parliament remained in the Arctic and continued his frustrating search for employment. In the four years since his days in Ottawa, Ittinuar had seen no full-time work other than sporadic research contracts for the Nunavut Constitutional Forum, the organization attempting to carve the Nunavut homeland out of the eastern half of the Northwest Territories. Job applications to the bureaucracies of the various Inuit organizations were turned down one after another. One rejection slip came from the Tungavik Federation of Nunavut, the group negotiating an Inuit land-claim settlement with the federal government. While he was not hired for an advertised negotiator's position, Ittinuar said he did help another person get the job by writing his resume for him.

For a while, Ittinuar tried his hand at being a self-employed businessman. With a cabin cruiser and some Atco trailers he planned to convert into a hotel, he set his eyes on the North's young but promising tourism industry. But the Rankin Inlet hamlet council revoked his business licence because the lot he wanted for his hotel was not zoned for commercial use. Ittinuar's career as an entrepreneur had not lasted long, and he soon filed for unemployment insurance.

"I am one Eskimo who has gone to university and I haven't got a job," he shrugged. "Nobody will hire me. People don't want to associate with a fallen down, beaten out former MP. Inuit organizations have a notion that because I was a Liberal MP, the Progressive Conservative government may look unfavourably at them for hiring me."

Nepotism is painfully obvious in Inuit organizations and the people running them are "psuedo-socialists," Ittinuar claimed. "Friends count for a lot. Qualifications based on skill and education mean nothing." If and when the Northwest Territories divides into two separate territories, the government of a sparsely-populated eastern Arctic territory could be highly corrupt, he said. "I'm almost afraid to live in a regime where you don't have a chance at getting a job unless you know somebody." And because discussions about where to draw a boundary line to divide the East and West have been "muddled to the point of permanent indecision," Ittinuar withdrew his personal support for the concept of territorial division. He made a political career out of persuading the federal government to divide the Territories, but as an "unemployed, self-thinking man," Ittinuar believed that a new northern territory would never be created. The costs involved in setting up a new territorial government would be too great, he said. Reminded that Brian Mulroney's Conservatives claimed to support division, Ittinuar cynically replied: "Yeah, so what?"

His limited contract work with the Nunavut Constitutional Forum included explaining to groups in the Arctic the merits of a proposed boundary line. And if Ittinuar were to represent the Inuit in elected office again, "I would fight for division because it is the wish of the majority of the constituents."

But in 1985, Ittinuar was not even able to muster enough votes to win a seat on the Rankin Inlet education authority. Local people said privately that Rankin Inlet was a better place when Peter Ittinuar lived in Ottawa. Some considered him arrogant, others feared his unpredictable temper. He had never been popular in Rankin Inlet. His election victories in 1979 and 1980 were without support from his home town.

Nunatsiaq was a cruel riding. Achieving political success meant abandoning the traditional Inuit values of collectivism and community. Ittinuar's successor, Thomas Suluk, could not handle the pressure any better and did not seek re-election in 1988. "In order for me to attempt to pressure the government into resolving issues, I have had to become involved in party politics. I adopted the ways of the dominant society in every sense of the word. I battled my fellow Inuit for the right to speak for them. In doing so I alienated many of them," Suluk said after a year in office. "Look at me. I'm wearing a three-piece suit, speaking to you in English when I would very much prefer to be speaking in Inuktitut."

Both Inuit members of Parliament had gone to Ottawa with high ideals to help their people. Both were left with their hopes crushed. But for Peter Ittinuar, the frustrations of Parliament were preferable to the dismal years following his 1984 election defeat. Another run for office was not out of the question. "I have education and experience, so I think I'm qualified."

In the spring of 1988, he ran for the presidency of the Inuit Tapirisat of Canada, the organization that represents the political and cultural interests of Canada's 20,000 Inuit. He lost. The defeat convinced Ittinuar to consider a career change. In the fall of 1988, the Canadian Broadcasting Corporation gave him his break and hired him as a radio broadcaster in Rankin Inlet.

In the media, Ittinuar could remain in the public's eye, but not have to depend on the public's vote.

PART III
BUSINESS LIVES

NICK LEBESSIS: FUR TRADER AND JET SETTER

An Inuit trapper stood motionless, staring at $4,000 in cash that he had just received for some pelts of white fox.

"Would you like anything else?" asked Nick Lebessis, the fur trader who made the deal.

"Yes," replied the trapper, who had never seen so much money. "A tea and a cigarette."

The pelts were sent to Winnipeg, where the manager of the fur auction was so impressed by their quality that he gave Lebessis an advance of $50,000 to buy more.

"Then I needed a tea and a cigarette," said the Greek-born trader.

Within a month, airplane loads of white fox were leaving Lebessis's home community of Eskimo Point, on the west coast of Hudson Bay, about 100 kilometers north of the Manitoba border. He soon cornered the market in the entire Keewatin region of the Northwest Territories. Trappers from communities 250 kilometers away would travel all day to sell their furs to Lebessis because he paid such high prices.

He would wake some mornings to find twenty-five trappers lined up outside his house. His wife would bring tea to the doorstep all day as he handed out $40 for each fox pelt. The Hudson's Bay Company, the only other game in town, paid $30, and usually only as credit for groceries or supplies.

Once, the Bay tried to force Lebessis out of business by raising its price to $60. He decided to "call their bluff" and raised his price to $100. "I thought I'd go for broke. I had nothing to lose."

Word travelled fast around the small Inuit settlement. Some trappers bought back furs that they had just sold to the Bay and took them to Lebessis. That lasted one afternoon before the Bay agreed to return to the original price structure.

Then one day in 1981, the Eskimo Point hamlet council wrote Lebessis a letter stating he was breaching hamlet by-laws by running a business out of his house. The concept of zoning a settlement had just been introduced to the North and it so happened that Lebessis's house was not in the commercial district. He showed the letter to the trappers who came by his house with furs to sell, and who then took over the next hamlet council meeting. The trappers forced the municipality to find a commercial lot for Lebessis' business. He received a small shack in the middle of a swamp, which was soon dubbed "Nick's Ark" because it had "a pelt of every animal."

Yet Lebessis realized that "the old times where you do your own thing in the North was over. I was fortunate to have been a part of it."

Lebessis was the last of the old-fashioned fur traders. He bought animal skins from the native people and sold them to the outside world — the same economic activity on which the country of Canada had been built.

Lebessis came to Canada in 1970 from Greece, after being expelled from one boarding school after another. After staying with his sister and brother-in-law in Ontario, he moved north in 1976 to work as a dishwasher in Frobisher Bay, where he met his wife, Rachael. In 1977, he returned to Greece for a visit and brought back a white fox pelt as a gift for another sister.

He stopped at a furrier in Athens to have the pelt fashioned into a collar. There he noticed a shawl made of two foxes selling for about $1,000.

He stopped in Paris on his way back to Canada, picked up some business cards and made promises that he could ship fox pelts directly from the North. Fortuitously, Rachael was offered a job in Eskimo Point, close to the richest supply of white fox in the Eastern Arctic.

Soon after his return to the North, Nick bought his first 50 pelts and was about to take them to Europe when his brother-in-law in Toronto "talked some sense" into him.

"Where the hell do you think you're going?" he asked Lebessis. "You don't have an export permit and you're not set up to carry on a business."

So Lebessis took his fox pelts to the furriers in downtown Toronto and "I was laughed at," he recalled. "I had paid $35 each for them and the most I was offered was $15."

The furriers complained that the pelts were not tanned, and so Lebessis found somebody who tanned the hides in his basement for $35 each. "By the time I was through, my first venture had put me in the hole by about $4,000. All my money was invested in 50 tanned foxes sitting in a bag."

Meanwhile, in 1979, the Lebessises went to Yellowknife where Rachael gave birth to their first child. Nick pedalled the fox furs on the city streets to pay for their return to Eskimo Point. "It was a very unpleasant situation," he said. "Life was saying that you're more or less a drifter and not only that, you're a lousy businessman too.

"My daughter was born underprivileged, but I made a promise to myself that my next child was going to be born into millions."

After returning to Eskimo Point, he decided he would try selling fox pelts through the Winnipeg fur auction. By that route, he quickly made a profit and his second of three children was born into "well, let's not say millions," he said, "but into affluence."

Before long, the market for trapped white fox collapsed because of the introduction of fox farms in other parts of the country and world. White fox bred on a ranch is better quality, twice the size and only a slightly higher price than wild fox. The market crash destroyed the local economy. Lebessis stopped buying furs from Eskimo Point trappers, but he had learned enough about the fur industry to take his business outside the Territories. That was when his business really boomed. In four years, his enterprise expanded from a floating shack in Eskimo Point to offices and warehouses across the country, manufacturing operations in Montreal and Toronto, and retail outlets in Thompson, Manitoba, and Yellowknife. Trading furs also provided a vehicle to deal Inuit art and by 1982 he had become a major distributor of Keewatin tapestries and soapstone carvings. His private corporate structure included five companies which fell under the parent firm, Dionne Furs, named after a lake near Eskimo Point. The companies employed 50 people, including a full-time lawyer, accountant and an agent in London.

Lebessis would sell and buy furs at auctions, and ship them to clients around the world. A typical week would involve catching a morning flight from Athens to Frankfurt, where he would spend a few hours with local furriers. He would then take an afternoon flight to Toronto and visit customers, factory workers and designers. There would be a night flight to Winnipeg and then on to Edmonton and Yellowknife the following day. He would fly to Eskimo Point for a few days and then back to Greece, via Winnipeg, Toronto, Montreal and London.

The people at the Greek village where Lebessis grew up did not believe that so much traveling was possible in one week. So for proof, Lebessis once took a hat that belonged to one of the doubters and brought it back to Eskimo Point. He took a picture of the hat on an iceberg in Hudson Bay and showed it to the astonished villagers a week later.

Eskimo Point was still home and Lebessis returned there every weekend. After sleeping in an igloo one Saturday night while out hunting, Lebessis came into town to find a message from a Canadian furrier who wanted some pelts purchased at the Monday fur auction in London. He took off the caribou skin clothing that he wore for hunting and put on a business suit. He chartered a small bush plane out of Eskimo Point and then flew first class from Winnipeg to London.

He purchased the furs in London and re-imported them to Canada. The fur business had become a global trade. As world prices fluctuated, Canadian furs were sold to Europe and bought from Europe, and then sometimes sold back to Europe again. "It used to be London buying furs from Eskimo Point," said Lebessis. "Now it's Eskimo Point buying furs from London."

Lebessis's entrance into the international fur market meant an admittance to an exclusive club. A member's word is good for any value of furs he wishes to trade; and along with the membership come more connections. It was not unusual for Lebessis to find himself in the company of Greek shipowners at a London night spot or with the Canadian establishment at a party in Montreal. He was once invited to a dinner for Queen Elizabeth, who was on a royal tour of Canada in 1984. He wrote off the $250 cost of renting a tuxedo as a business expense. It was the only item Revenue Canada questioned when he became the first person in the Eastern Arctic to have his income tax audited. Lebessis told the auditors that it was a gift to the Queen; gifts to the Queen are tax-exempt. "I had a good accountant," he said. Lebessis was young (in his early 30s), a bit of a charmer, and well acquainted with the ways of both the Europeans and North Americans. But he was popular with the "jet set" mostly because he was a novelty — he came from the North. "Who else there could have claimed that they were from Eskimo Point in the Northwest Territories and still be able to catch the same flight to Frankfurt tomorrow as they did?" he asked. "I'm not saying I had their money or their social status, but I had the same lifestyle. I was where they were, but they could never be where I was. They could never take a flight to Eskimo Point the next day and sleep in an igloo and hunt and eat raw meat and raw fish. I was a curiosity in that way."

The jet set often asked why he bothered to stay in the Arctic.

"There is no justified reason for me to be in the North because my Jaguar cars are parked in the South," he said. "But my love isn't exclusive to money. The North is where I had the opportunity to realize my potential. I belong here. My wife is an Inuk and my children were born here, so I can never escape the North."

Yet Lebessis no longer buys furs from the North because, he said, "I wouldn't even be making minimum wage." So while he has prospered, other residents of Eskimo Point have struggled. They now trap for recreation rather than commerce. At about the same time the white fox market collapsed, the demand for the Inuit's only other fur product — sealskin — faded because of boycotts staged by animal rights groups. In 1981, an Inuit hunter could sell a seal pelt for $20. Three years later, he was lucky to get six dollars. The anti-fur lobby hurts the harvesters of wild fur more than anyone, especially the native people of the Arctic where the only saleable furs were seal and whitefox. The economic devastation helped create a depressed society dependent on welfare cheques.

While the animal rights movement destroys the native people, it has not affected other components of the fur industry, Lebessis said. "I have the option to manufacture mink instead of seal. And I can always market in Asia where the demand for fur is growing. There are a billion Chinese to do business with."

Once Lebessis came face-to-face with a demonstrator outside the London fur auction. As he tells the story, she held a drawing of a seal's head with its eyes emphasized in joy, and a slogan that read: "Their eyes are innocent. Don't kill them."

She charged Lebessis and told him that he was "killing for profit."

"Have you ever visited an Eskimo village?" he asked her.

"What's that got to do with anything?"

"If you could visit one, you would notice the children. Their eyes are innocent too." He then started to walk away.

"We'll send them food, if they need food."

Lebessis turned around and said: "Then you'll call them welfare bums."

"They can do something else."

"What? Raise cows? Or grow potatoes?"

After the confrontation, Lebessis concluded that those involved in the anti-fur movement were "in another dimension." But, he said, they should not be taken lightly. "We should not be fooled when Greenpeace says it won't fight the fur industry (as it said in 1986). It's not that they don't want to fight it, it's just that they have more important things to deal with such as nuclear disarmament. They can do that without any opposition whatsoever. I mean, we're all for nuclear disarmament. Even Reagan and Gorbachev are for it, so who's left?"

Since most people still eat farmed meat without a guilty conscience, it has been suggested that the ranching of domestic animals rather than the trapping of wild ones is also the answer for the fur industry. Fur farming throws the argument back at the animal rights groups: "A farmed animal experiences the gift of life, as short as it may be, because it serves an economic purpose," said Lebessis. "If that demand for the fur did not exist, neither would this animal."

There are very few fur farms in northern Canada despite the collapse in wild fur markets. The lack of aboriginal land-claims settlements has hampered such developments; the Inuit argue a political base must accompany an economic base. Some also say that Inuit culture is based on a life among animals running freely in the wide-open spaces of the wilderness, not in captivity on a farm. But native people adjusted to shooting animals with guns rather than arrows and they would eventually adjust to farm life as well, Lebessis said. "Native people have a natural gift and feeling for animals, wherever they are."

He pointed to the native people who made the transition in Siberia and Lapland. Together, the Scandinavian countries now export $10 billion worth of ranched fur every year — the same amount as Canadian lumber exports.

While he is a prime advocate of fur farms in the North, Lebessis is not about to start one himself. He is already Eskimo Point's wealthiest person and largest employer, next to the government. If he were to start a farm, local people would think it was "so Nick can have foxes to sell around the world," he said. "My opinion is really for the benefit of the industry at large, not myself."

Besides, by 1986 Lebessis was more concerned with spending time with his family than with expanding his corporate empire. "Shaping the lives of your own children is more important than shaping the future of your businesses," he said. "It's a realization that comes with the years, through maturity. I draw my greatest pleasure in sliding down the hill with my children in Eskimo Point and knowing the world out there is something that I can conquer if I want to."

The jet set, however, should not forget the curiosity from the North. Once his children are grown up, Lebessis said, "I will roll up my sleeves and get ready for another round."

WILLIAM NASOGALUAK: REINDEER ARE NOT CARIBOU

William Nasogaluak would rather round up reindeer than lawyers, but for him the two seem to go together.

During the 1980s, meat from Canada's only commercial reindeer herd near Tuktoyaktuk, N.W.T., wound up in restaurants and food markets around the world. And reindeer antlers were shipped to the Orient for medicinal purposes, including use as an aphrodisiac. What had once been a money-losing government experiment had become a thriving northern-based agricultural industry. But instead of thanking the man who made it all happen, two levels of government and a powerful aboriginal organization worked to edge Nasogaluak out of the North's economic picture.

The first reindeer in North America had been brought from Siberia to Alaska in the 1890s. In 1929, the Canadian government bought 3,000 of the Alaskan reindeer to provide the Inuvialuit with employment and food, as much of the caribou in the area had been wiped out by whalers at the turn of the century. The reindeer did not always cooperate on the famous trek to the Tuktoyaktuk Peninsula. They tended to turn around and head back towards Alaska whenever they encountered storms and difficult river crossings. It took three years for the reindeer and their descendants to reach their new home.

When they arrived, the government planned to set up family farms and give one thousand reindeer and a grazing area to each household. That was the system used to raise reindeer in Lapland, in northern Scandinavia, and three families of Laplanders were brought to Tuktoyaktuk to teach the Inuvialuit the new skill of animal husbandry. Herding was a considerable adjustment for the native people who were used to hunting animals. The various owners competed for grazing lands and there were disputes over the ownership of the reindeer during round-up time. By the early 1960s, thirty years after the reindeer first arrived, the herd was costing Ottawa about $80,000 a year. So a university professor who had transplanted a herd of muskoxen from the Northwest Territories to the State of Vermont and the manager of the Alberta Game Farm near Edmonton were hired to operate the reindeer herd together. That did not work either. The two men could not get along and both were preoccupied with their other projects.

By 1974, Silas Kangegana, who had been a local work-hand and reindeer herder for twenty years, suggested that the herders be given a chance to run the reindeer business. The government loaned Kangegana some money and sold him the herd for $40,000. But the business caused Kangegana much stress and, after suffering a heart attack, he decided to sell the animals. Eunice Nasogaluak, Kangegana's niece, was keeping the books for the reindeer business at the time, and her husband William had usually helped with the round-up. Kangegana said he would sell the herd only to Nasogaluak. In 1978, Nasogaluak bought the herd for $250,000 and agreed to pay Kangegana a fixed annual amount for 10 years.

Nasogaluak had spent twenty years in Tuktoyaktuk working as a mechanic and heavy equipment operator. He took over a herd of 10,000 reindeer, and there were many experienced herders in Tuktoyaktuk, but the business had never earned a profit. He built a portable slaughter house that was pulled by a front-end loader across the barrenlands to where the reindeer were grazing. A carcass went in one end and meat came out the other. The facility was approved by the federal Department of Agriculture, which meant reindeer steaks and roasts could be sold in southern Canada and eventually around the world. Before, reindeer meat had been sold only in the North.

Reindeer meat sold on the international market for $2.30 per pound during most of 1980s. (Locally, it went for eighty-five cents.) About 3,500 animals were slaughtered in an average year, producing about 500,000 pounds of meat. Reindeer became increasingly popular as a health food. It is an extremely lean meat, for those concerned with cholesterol, and it has no growth hormones or other additives. The reindeer roamed freely on the tundra and scraped off moss, lichen and grass for food.

They were rounded up for the slaughter each February, when the daylight returns to the Arctic coast and when it is still cold enough to store the meat outside. About forty people from Tuktoyaktuk were hired seasonally to help corral the animals. The event looked like a western-style cattle round-up, except instead of horses, the modern-day herders used helicopters and snowmobiles to guide the animals into pens.

Nasogaluak also received inquiries about reindeer antlers and soon there was another round-up in the summer for a "horn harvest." Every year, herders sawed off 20,000 pounds of antlers, which fetched between $15 and $55 per pound. At first, it seemed ridiculous that people would pay so much for something which Nasogaluak thought had no value. He took the money, but did not let his business become dependant on the antler sales because it was a market he could not control and did not understand.

The use of reindeer antlers as an aphrodisiac receives the most attention, but the application is much wider. In the Far East — Korea particularly — the antlers are ground into a powder and sold through apothecary shops as an ingredient for traditional medicines. Oriental medicines also required hoofs, tails, belly buttons, penises and leg skins. And North American pharmaceutical companies bought the reindeer livers, while tongues have always been a local delicacy.

The potential for the reindeer herd seemed endless and beyond imagination. Plans for a new generation of portable slaughter houses were off the drawing board and Nasogaluak considered buying a couple of helicopters to complement the small airplane that he already had to monitor the reindeer. There was talk about splitting the herd and creating new operations in other parts of the North. But all future plans were put on hold, and eventually shelved, when Nasogaluak was forced out of business.

The origins of his problems dated back a long time. In 1955, about 50,000 square kilometres had been set aside for the then government-owned herd, and in 1974, when the reindeer were handed to private enterprise, Ottawa had promised to "continue to make such a provision for the grazing of a reindeer herd." For Nasogaluak, the pressure started in 1984, when the federal government reached a native land-claim settlement with the Inuvialuit, the Inuit who live around the Beaufort Sea in the Western Arctic. The 3,000 Inuvialuit received $78 million and title to 91,000 square kilometers of land, including a portion that intersects the reindeer grazing reserve. However, the 115-page document that detailed the Inuvialuit land-claim agreement made no provision for reindeer grazing. The federal government lost sight of its commitment after negotiations between the government, the Inuvialuit and Nasogaluak fell apart.

"They wouldn't listen to what I was telling them. If people want to make mistakes, I don't want to be a part of it," said Nasogaluak, who is an Inuvialuit himself and eligible to benefit from the land-claim settlement.

Federal land-claim negotiator Simon Reisman, the former deputy minister of finance who would go on to negotiate Canada's free-trade agreement with the United States, said that there was a "carefully calculated plan" to deal with the 15,000 reindeer. Nasogaluak thought that the plan was to force him to sell the herd to the Inuvialuit.

The Inuvialuit Regional Corporation offered $1.3 million for the herd. Its appraised value in 1983 was $4.9 million.

"I'm not going to give it away," responded Nasogaluak. "If they were serious about it, I would talk." Inuvialuit leaders said that they did their own analysis and called the price "fair."

Shortly after the land-claim was settled, the Northwest Territories government's minister of renewable resources, Nellie Cournoyea, who also is an influential Inuvialuit politician and was one of their land-claim negotiators, changed wildlife hunting regulations to permit the hunting of caribou on the reindeer reserve. The size of Nasogaluak's herd was reduced by hunters who mistook the reindeer for caribou. No reindeer meat was produced after 1985 because the 3,500 reindeer that were usually slaughtered each year were instead being poached.

The Inuvialuit corporation then told Nasogaluak to pay access fees for the use of their land. The fuss was over a ten-mile strip of tundra the reindeer crossed twice a year while moving between a winter grazing range of moss and lichen on the Tuktoyaktuk Peninsula and a grassy summer range further inland. Nasogaluak did not pay the bills. Their permit would have dictated where the animals had to graze, how many could be slaughtered, where and to whom the meat had to be sold, and it provided no safeguards against poaching.

The Inuvialuit filed a court action against Nasogaluak in December 1986 to remove the herd from its land and to seek damages for trespassing. The Supreme Court of the Northwest Territories refused the corporation a temporary injunction for the immediate removal of the reindeer. But Nasogaluak saw himself in the middle of a "squeeze play" as the people who would not offer a fair price for the purchase of his reindeer were the same ones who were evicting the animals from the land that they have grazed since 1932. So he decided to look for a buyer outside the Territories. A deal was struck in 1986 to send 15,000 live reindeer — the entire herd — to the Peoples' Republic of China. Nasogaluak received two export permits — one from the federal government and one from the Northwest Territories government. Then a territorial government official "received instructions" to tell Nasogaluak that the Northwest Territories permit was invalid and that he could not export the live animals. The permit supposedly had the wrong expiry date and the government should have charged a fee of five dollars for each animal, for a total of $75,000.

Nasogaluak was never charged a fee in previous years when he had shipped smaller numbers of live reindeer to zoos and private game farms. And he usually only had a federal permit. This time he had applied for a territorial one "as an additional measure."

The territorial permit was based on the Northwest Territories government's authority to regulate northern wildlife. Nasogaluak took the government to the Supreme Court of the Northwest Territories, arguing that his reindeer were not "wildlife." They were domesticated, just like cattle, he said. "Reindeer are a tranquil and gentle animal which tend to congregate together and remain content wherever forage is good."

The government lawyer said that reindeer are wild animals in their natural environment in northern Europe. As such, he argued, reindeer and caribou are essentially the same thing. The Supreme Court judge said that people would want to know for certain if there was a difference, "especially children at Christmas time."

The reindeer versus caribou debate had seen its day in court before. In 1948, a hunter charged with poaching on the Tuktoyaktuk reindeer herd entered the defence that he thought he was shooting caribou. Expert witnesses said then that reindeer are a lighter colour than the caribou's various shades of brown. And caribou run away when chased. Reindeer run in circles, which makes them easy to pen at round-up time. In other words, reindeer were not "wildlife" in the same sense that caribou were.

In another case, in 1982, meat markets in Montreal that sold Nasogaluak's reindeer meat were charged under provincial regulations forbidding the sale of wildlife. There was confusion in Quebec because there is no separate word in French for "reindeer" and the animals are both called "caribou." The Quebec court ruled that, while reindeer are a sub-species of caribou, there is in fact a difference.

As Nasogaluak's case entered its second day on May 27, 1987, the lawyers announced in the Yellowknife courtroom that the territorial government had backed down. Realizing that the precedents were against them, the government had decided over night that reindeer were not wild after all. For Nasogaluak, it was a bittersweet victory. The Chinese ended up buying red deer from New Zealand while the reindeer dispute was tied up in court.

Nasogaluak started to negotiate with other potential buyers. A deal to send the herd to Alberta fell through after the provincial government there refused to grant import permits. It was worried that the reindeer might carry parasites which did not affect the meat, but could spread to cattle. Nasogaluak said that he would slaughter the entire herd and sell the meat if the animals could not be sold alive. That would have meant an end to the Canadian reindeer industry. But eventually a deal was struck with a group of Hong Kong investors who wanted to ranch the herd in the Peace River area of northern British Columbia. The B.C. government also tested the reindeer for parasites, but it approved their importation. Plans were made to truck the reindeer herd out of the Northwest Territories in 1989. Nasogaluak would not say how much the Hong Kong group was willing to pay for the live herd, but it was more than the earlier estimated value of $4.9 million.

By 1988, the reindeer rancher did not talk much about the herd and was unsure of his future plans. The soft-spoken man did not want to be interviewed for this book because "it's a sad story." But, he said to "go ahead" and write about him anyway.

Many people considered the scheme to force the sale of the herd to the Inuvialuit corporation as nothing more than an attempt to grab a successful business venture. The government and Inuvialuit leaders thought the pressure on Nasogaluak would be too great as he started to run out of money. They underestimated his wealth, but to Nasogaluak, that was not the point. He vowed not to be bullied, even if it meant an end to a prosperous farming industry that was unique to the North and envied by the rest of Canada.

DOUG BILLINGSLEY: PLAYING DIFFERENT ROLES

You do not need a PhD to run a hardware store, but Doug Billingsley has one anyway. Then again, the Inuvik entrepreneur had the smarts to get into business at a time when most others in Inuvik, N.W.T., were pulling out.

Billingsley was in charge of the government's regional economic development office in Inuvik before he went into private business in 1978. His government duties included encouraging people with various incentives and loan funds to take advantage of business opportunities in the area.

"I spent three years with a good staff and a generous budget trying to draw these opportunities to people's attention, and those were good years, optimistic years," said Billingsley. "I couldn't get people to take advantage of what was here. I was getting pretty frustrated. I came to the conclusion that it wasn't possible for me to do that job."

Billingsley had gone to work for the Northwest Territories government because he could not find a job anywhere else. In 1973, after receiving his doctorate in resource geography, specializing in atmospheric pollution, at the University of Edinburgh, he returned to Canada and found that the universities were not hiring.

"You have to feed your family," he said. "It was really a matter of using whatever skills and abilities I had."

While growing up in the Muskoka area of Ontario, Billingsley would tag along with his father, who was a building contractor, on his rounds to check boiler rooms and fix broken doors and windows. Now Doug, accompanied by his dog, Sandhurst, does the same thing in Inuvik that his father did in Ontario.

"The irony is that my father told me, 'son, you've got to get an education so you won't have to work as hard as I've worked. Get one of those good jobs and you're going to have a better life than I had.

"So I said, 'yes sir' and I went off and did those things, but when the wheel came around, I was faced with no work and a family and the things I fell back on were the things that Dad taught me."

In the late 1970s in Inuvik, Doug and Vicki Billingsley "bought everything we could manage to buy," Doug said with a laugh. "It was a funny kind of time."

Almost half of its 4,400 people had left town, after a plan to construct a natural gas pipeline down the Mackenzie River Valley was put on hold to allow time for the settlement of native land-claims. The active search for oil and gas in the Beaufort Sea and Mackenzie River delta, on which Inuvik's economy relied, came to a halt. As the boom went bust, the Billingsleys bought office buildings and warehouses with no money down and no interest charges. They bought retail outlets for just the cost of the inventory. They eventually owned over thirty properties and businesses in Inuvik. They were convinced that the oil companies would eventually return. They were right, and sure enough the town's economy improved. If a person now wants retail or office space in Inuvik, he talks to Doug Billingsley.

Dome Petroleum carried Inuvik's economy for the first few years Billingsley was in business. Backed by government incentive grants, Dome was the only oil company that stayed to look for oil in the Beaufort Sea. Conscious of its corporate image, it spent money freely on building hockey arenas, establishing a local vocational training school, and even sponsoring annual whale surveys to determine the effects of its off-shore drill rigs on the creatures' migration paths. Dome shares were then doubling every year and people in Inuvik, where the nearest stockbroker was 2,000 kilometers away, invested heavily.

"We were all in that game," said Billingsley. "It was almost an item of religious faith that you could depend on Dome Petroleum. Looking back, we expected too much from Dome."

By 1984, the company was caught with a large debt at high interest rates and declining world oil prices. The stock prices tumbled and, like Dome itself, many investors in Inuvik never recovered. Soon Dome's Beaufort Sea operations shut down. The other oil companies had returned to pick up the slack, but they scaled down yet again in 1986. Inuvik businessmen were learning all about the boom-and-bust cycle of the oil industry.

The next time the oil companies come back, they will want to finally build a pipeline to transport the Beaufort oil. Many northern businessmen look forward to that day because then the companies will have to stay and drill for oil to feed their pipeline. But Billingsley is worried about the dramatic impact the construction of such a mega-project would have on the North. "I don't even want to be here then," he said. "Slow and steady, that's the best. This boom-bust stuff is really hard. I'm not arguing for government intervention — I wouldn't go that far — but the longer the construction phase could be spread out, the better."

Aboriginal land-claims are no longer a great impediment for Beaufort oil and gas development. The Inuvialuit, the Inuit of the Western Arctic, received 91,000 square kilometers and $78 million from the federal government in a 1984 land-claim settlement. The Inuvialuit favoured a pipeline, so long as they were in on the action. They invested their land-claim money into oil and gas developments, a barging and trucking company, a regional airline, and various business enterprises and construction projects. Most of them are based in Inuvik.

The Inuvialuit's investments boosted the local economy in the late 1980s, just as Dome had done a decade earlier. Inuvialuit organizations even took over the office space that Dome had previously occupied. Billingsley was the landlord for both. The Inuvialuit organizations also displaced the oil companies as his best customer at the hardware store and lumber yard.

Yet Billingsley has had on-going disputes with Inuvialuit leaders over other matters. The most publicized involved William Nasogaluak's reindeer herding enterprise for which Billingsley acted as a business advisor. At times, the herd grazed on land acquired by the Inuvialuit in their land-claim settlement and the native group was trying to evict the animals. Billingsley often criticized Inuvialuit leaders for their "stupidity" as they "go to such great lengths to destroy the viability" of the North's unique farming industry.

"You say it's a little two-faced," he said, "but one of the true aspects of life in the North is that there are so few people and you are all playing different roles. You have to develop an ability to disagree and remain friends because there's so much politics here, particularly with the land-claim, that this community could be fractured if everybody stayed rigidly in their group roles."

Billingsley has five times played the role of president of the Inuvik Chamber of Commerce. Under his direction, the chamber often espoused causes and took positions that were not popular with business groups in other parts of the North. In fact, the Inuvik chamber opposed government policies that were designed to protect northern firms. It once called for the resignation of the Northwest Territories' minister of economic development because of the "inconsiderate" manner in which he handed out government grants to create new businesses that competed with existing ones. The chamber also rejected a policy to give northern businesses a preference over southern firms when handing out government contracts. If anything, Inuvik entrepreneurs said, the policy would prevent local businesses from expanding. It would discourage new investment in the North and stifle joint ventures between northern and southern companies.

"We tried to argue for fairness, particularly in tendering procedures, to get away from a situation where preference was given to one group and against others, and to let the market place and the bidding process dictate who gets what," Billingsley said.

In the North, preference is usually given to native people, who are the majority but who also live at the lower end of the economic scale. An affirmative action policy of the territorial government designed to increase the number of natives in the civil service and on contract to the government, was adamantly protested by the Inuvik chamber. The chamber wanted the policy to have a "sunset clause" so the government would revert to regular hiring practices once the targeted number of natives in the workforce had been reached. "Otherwise it's just entrenching a racial preference," Billingsley said.

The government also tried to discriminate against white people, he maintained, when a territorial-wide plebiscite was held in 1982 to see if Northerners wanted to divide the Northwest Territories into two separate territories. Only people who lived in the Northwest Territories for more than three years were allowed to vote. Doug and Vicki Billingsley and ten others challenged the validity of the plebiscite in the Supreme Court of the Northwest Territories, claiming that it denied short-term residents of their mobility rights and their freedom to express their views "on matters of importance."

The Billingsleys lost the court case, but the judge ruled that the three-year residency requirement would have been unreasonable if it had been an election rather than a plebiscite. The vote to divide the territories was considered to be similar to an opinion poll of a certain group and not binding on the legislature.

"It was that little rider that established you can't get away with back door discrimination. It was good to see the court recognized what was going on," Billingsley said. "But it shouldn't have fallen to my wife and me to have to do that and to have to pay for that. That cost us a lot of money.

"The government was unfair then. This is what's so disturbing about the territorial government. They play favourites. A public government ought not to do that, but they do... We have a government that can't react to you unless it knows what race you are. It's a racial labelling process — you're a Metis, you're an Indian, you're an Eskimo, or you're an 'other.' It has to ask which one you are before it knows what services it will give you. I think that is a bad situation."

If "racist" government policies made his life insufferable, Billingsley would leave the North. But "I don't want to be pushed aside by processes that I perceive to be evil, and I perceive a substantial part of what the territorial government does as evil."

As he was not about to "cut and run," Billingsley would stick it out in Inuvik for a while longer and look after his office buildings, hardware store and lumber yard.

JOHN TODD: THE JOINT VENTURE

One way to succeed in business in the North is to involve as many native people as possible and get to know the politicians who hand out government contracts. It has worked for John Todd, and he makes no apologies for it.

"To me, it's just the normal North American way: you get out there and lobby and go kiss babies and whatever it takes. If others don't want to do it, that's their problem," said the Scottish-born businessman who came north as a teenager to work for the Hudson's Bay Company.

Todd now has investments across the Northwest Territories, all of them with partners, many of whom are Inuit. "I don't want to sound melodramatic, but I think we have an intense involvement with native people. I hope it's not paternalistic. I don't think it is. It's just good business and they're friends. They're good friends. Period.

"You can't be successful alone. There's the danger that you'd then become a lonely, isolated person."

The Northwest Territories government encourages joint ventures between northern natives and white businessmen and "a lot of people are doing it today because it is the 'in' thing," Todd said. "We did it because it was the right thing."

In 1974, Todd and a school principal set up Siniktarvik Limited and sold company shares to about two dozen local people — Inuit and white. They raised enough money to buy a hotel in Rankin Inlet, in the Keewatin region of the Northwest Territories.

"It was an intimate exercise with the shareholders," Todd said. "They were involved in everything. Everybody would bust their ass. The whole sweat equity thing with everyone pitching in for nothing was so important. They'd contribute in any way. They'd clean, they'd cook when the cook was sick."

All the shareholders had other full-time jobs, so there was no need to pay out dividends. The profits were reinvested. By 1988, Siniktarvik, which in Inuktitut, means "a place where people come to sleep," had grown to include not only the Rankin Inlet hotel, but also a hotel in Frobisher Bay, a construction company, a real estate firm and a travel agency. Todd has been the company's chief executive officer for the past decade.

Most of the $20 million in revenues the businesses generate every year come from government contracts. Conferences and meetings are often held at the hotels, and each delegate spends over $100 a night to sleep there. Rankin Inlet is a regional administrative centre and the government rents much of its office space from John Todd. He also receives many construction contracts to build public housing. "We've always been politically active," Todd said. "We went out there to get people elected to the legislative assembly who were going to represent our interests. And when you get people elected, you ask them for favours, that's the way it is."

The two Keewatin MLAs in office for most of the 1980s were Tagak Curley, who had John Todd as his campaign manager for two elections, and Gordon Wray, another Scotsman who came to work for the Hudson's Bay Company. Both MLAs held important economic portfolios in the territorial cabinet. Todd always kept in close contact, reminding them that "the sun doesn't rise and set in Yellowknife, it sets in the Keewatin, and we want some attention and we want some change." He usually got it.

In 1980, he set up the Keewatin Chamber of Commerce with a $10,000 grant from the Northwest Territories government. The region's business community now had a legitimate lobby group rather than having people think "it's just John Todd flapping his gums."

Todd was its president and official spokesman for the first three years, and he is still the group's "unofficial" spokesman. The chamber is not an exclusive club of businessmen who seek their privacy. Its annual general meetings — which are always held at the Siniktarvik Hotel in Rankin Inlet — are extravagant public affairs that include evening entertainment by nationally renowned performers such as John Allen Cameron. The chamber, or at least John Todd, takes the same lavish approach when lobbying the government.

"People lobby in different ways," Todd said. "Some people do it subtly, some people do it quietly, some people do it aggressively and loud. I decided to do it aggressively and loud because I wanted attention. I wanted people to sit up and listen to what we were saying."

Given the hectic pace he sets, it is not surprising that Todd has not had much of a family life. He has been married twice and has fathered four children over 18 years. "I must admit, my domestic life has been one of my failings," he said. "I suppose I should have spent more time on that, but you become so damn consumed in what you're doing."

Todd is short and squat, yet his presence cannot be missed. With a thick Scottish accent, his speech is flamboyant and exaggerated. He likes to get a reaction. "I found that if you say 'fuck', everybody listens. It stirs up such a dramatic effect on people. So I say 'fuck' a lot."

His abrasive manner has offended government bureaucrats and businessmen in other parts of the North, particularly in the relatively more sophisticated city of Yellowknife. "But that's their fuckin' problem, not mine," he said. "I thought, 'fuck you guys.' I'm not out there representing Yellowknife, I haven't got any investments there."

The foul language Todd now uses in just about every sentence were words he had "never heard" before coming north. He learned them quickly in his younger years while working at the Bay and at a Yellowknife gold mine. Drinking and violence, "especially on paydays," were part of everyday life at the bunk houses where he and the other single men of the workplace lived.

The Hudson's Bay Company drew Todd north in 1965, when he was eighteen years old. He answered a newspaper advertisement in the Dundee *Courier* calling for young men seeking an "adventure in the Canadian North." He arrived in the Central Arctic community of Cambridge Bay wearing a new suit and tie and was put straight to work unloading boxes of meat from the airplane. Blood dripped all over his new clothes. He unloaded planes, stocked shelves and mopped floors for the Bay for only six months, but deep down Todd still thinks of himself as a "Bay Boy," as do many other Scots who worked for the company and have since become among the North's most prominent businessmen, politicians and civil servants.

"When we all get together and have a few drinks, the Bay's all we talk about," Todd said.

Realizing that he was "being exploited" by the company, Todd moved to Yellowknife to make more money working in one of the local gold mines. In 1970, he was hired by the Northwest Territories government to help set up a municipal government in Cambridge Bay. In 1972, he was transferred to Rankin Inlet and fell in love with the flat, wind-swept community. It was the people who made the difference.

"They were more aggressive and had an individual initiative that I hadn't seen elsewhere in the North. It made my job a lot easier."

During 1973, Todd did not do "a hell of a lot of work. It was the most irresponsible year that I've ever had in my life. There were guys drinking, there were guys doing drugs, there were guys doing other guys' wives. It was nuts. It was chaos. Guys would turn off another guy's oil in the middle of the night just to bug the hell out of him. There must have been something in the air."

He did not want to leave Rankin Inlet, but he was promoted in 1975 to a job in Frobisher Bay, on Baffin Island. "You're moving up the ladder, you're making more money and you have to act like a goddamn bureaucrat. In retrospect, it was pretty stifling. The whole motivation was to get out."

To make matters worse, he did not get along with his superiors. "I'm a pretty abrasive son-of-a-bitch, as most people know, but it wasn't a question of sticking your finger up to authority, it was a question of going out and doing your own thing."

He received an educational leave — "I think it was the fastest approval for educational leave in the history of the territorial government" — but instead of going to school, he went to Yellowknife to work for Polar Gas, an energy conglomerate that wanted to build natural gas pipelines to southern Canada from the Beaufort Sea and the High Arctic. When he suggested a joint venture with the Inuit, his boss at the time responded: "Bullshit, absolute bullshit."

Todd was summoned to Toronto to see the vice-president, who said: "I hear that you're anti-pipeline."

"I don't know what the hell I am," Todd answered. "But I do know there's a lot of emotion out there and I don't think you guys are realizing it. You had better deal with the emotion or it's going to cause you a lot of problems."

During the mid 1970s, oil companies faced a strong aboriginal lobby that opposed the development of the North. "There was paranoia in the industry; you were either left or right. There was no in-the-middle," said Todd. "You were either a Commie or a Capitalist, so I had difficulty with that job."

He worked on community relations and a local training programme that the company would present to federal agencies when seeking approval to build the pipelines. None of the engineers, scientists and academics in the company would listen to Todd. He would say, for example, that if they wanted their caribou counts to have credibility in the eyes of the native people, they should take along the president of the local Hunters and Trappers Association in the helicopter. But, they would say it was a scientific exercise and would be carried out on a scientific basis, and that no Inuit hunter would be allowed to come along for a ride. Then they would return from a count and say: "Yea, there's lots of caribou out there." Since wildlife is such an emotional issue in the North, the native people would reply: "We don't believe you." Then Todd would take a perverse delight in telling the company people: "Here you are with all this intelligence and academic background and I'm just a little Bay clerk and you're stupid and I'm not."

After feeling out of place with Polar Gas, Todd returned to Rankin Inlet in 1977 to run Siniktarvik, where his business philosophy of involving the community was appreciated.

Many people in the Keewatin have since learned the ropes from Todd. In 1986, the government of the Northwest Territories leased twenty-three apartment units from a new northern company called Iligiitut Limited. When asked in the legislature why others did not have an opportunity to bid on the $2.2 million contract, the minister of public works — Gordon Wray — said that special treatment was given to native-owned businesses to encourage native people to get into private business.

Iligiitut's shareholders included three local Inuit and John Todd. After a week of further political debate over what constituted a "native-owned business," ten more Inuit were added to the shareholder list, at least one of whom denied ever being asked to participate in the company, and Todd's name was dropped. However, Todd remained involved with the company as a "consultant."

White businessmen from across the North have accused Todd of trying to make a buck for himself off the backs of the Inuit, or as one competing contractor said: "One of the reasons I am failing as a businessman is because I am not using a native word and native names to mislead the public and government."

"When you're as outspoken as I am, you're going to create a lot of enemies," Todd said.

As the people who have learned from Todd set out on their own and lobby the government themselves, their mentor hopes that "they're not all going to be John Todds. My God no, my ego's not that big." A variety of styles are needed, he said. "The political lobby isn't one person. It's a network where everyone contributes in different ways."

As for Todd himself and the approach he takes to business, he says bluntly: "I'm not about to change."

ED KLAUS: THE ARCTIC FREEWAY

"Fast" Eddie Klaus is a trucker whose 18 wheels never touch pavement.

His road is made of ice and snow. It crosses 650 kilometers of sub-arctic forest and wind-swept tundra, north from Yellowknife to a remote gold mine. It would take seven hours to drive the distance on a highway anywhere else in North America. It takes Klaus twenty-four hours, and that is when he is making good time.

The road to the Lupin mine crosses frozen lakes plowed as wide as a football field is long, and land portages of packed snow. On the lakes, the trucks create waves under the ice when they travel too fast. The waves buckle over when they reach shore, forcing the ice to break. A couple of trucks usually fall through the ice each winter — always close to shore.

Klaus "took a bath" in the winter of 1988. "It wasn't that bad, just the trailer went through. We used three trucks to winch it out. It came out pretty good, but we lost a whole day," he said. "You can't worry about going through. If you're going to worry, you shouldn't be on the ice."

Echo Bay Mines Limited, the Edmonton-based company that builds the road to its mine each winter, has patrol cars with radar guns that track down speeding truckers. (The limit is thirty mph for fully loaded trucks, forty-five mph when empty.) They are always looking out for Fast Eddie. The nickname does not help. Yet he earned it more for his stamina than a heavy foot. A secretary at a propane dealer came up with the name after Klaus had delivered thirty-four loads of propane in one month from Hay River over 500 kilometers of gravel road to Yellowknife and back. "In no time at all it just kind of travelled all over the country," Klaus said. "There are a lot of people who don't even know me by my right name."

Edward Klaus has been driving trucks since 1955, when he was sixteen years old. He was hauling logs in British Columbia and northern Alberta when, in 1969, he heard that a new sawmill at Fort Resolution, on the south shore of Great Slave Lake, was looking for drivers. He made nearby Hay River his permanent home in 1973. "When I first came here, I didn't like this country because stuff was hard to get. In civilization there, you could get parts for the truck the same day you needed them. Here you have to get it flown out or bussed up. I didn't like that. But I got used to it and then this place seemed like not so bad of a place to live. There was a lot of work around at that time. And the money was good."

Truck drivers are paid by the load, about $600 for each delivery to the Lupin mine. Klaus has made ninety-six Yellowknife-to-Lupin return trips from 1982, when the road opened, to 1987. He often makes two dozen trips a winter. Less than twenty is the normal for most truckers. He can afford to live year round on his winter's wage.

Klaus does not stop to rest much in the winter. "I have all spring to sleep," he said. "When a guy gets on the winter roads, he puts in a lot of hours because he only has three months to do it."

While his truck is being loaded in Yellowknife, Klaus grabs a shower, phones his wife in Hay River, and is then on his way back to the mine. "A lot of truckers want to go uptown. Not me. I'm worried about getting in as much work as I can."

Also in keeping with his reputation and nickname, Klaus does not waste time at either of the two service camps along the road where truckers can stop to eat and sleep. He will not wait for a meal, not even if a hot pot roast is about to come out of the oven. "I'd just make a sandwich, then be gone right away," he said. "Other guys will sit around for a couple of hours at mealtimes, or sit around and drink coffee and talk."

Klaus gets into a routine where he will sleep from midnight to 5 a.m. and spend almost every waking hour behind the wheel. Extra winks can wait for a snowstorm. When stranded on the unforgiving tundra, there is little else to do but crawl into the sleeper at the back of the cab and wait for the weather to clear.

Klaus's 200-gallon gas tank is large enough to keep his truck running — and him warm — for three days. The motor is wrapped in a tarpaulin to help keep the Arctic wind out, and by banking snow up the wheel-wells, he can cut down his idle and save fuel. But if a storm is approaching, he is more apt to step on it and try at least to reach the next camp. "A few times there I went through storms and there were snow drifts as high as the fenders on the truck. They were coming at me and I was trying to get out of Lupin mine. I was always lucky enough to make it."

At a camp, he can wait out a storm in comfort. He can eat well and watch satellite television. Or he may get stuck at the mine site if a storm moves in while his truck is being unloaded. Then he may take a tour of the underground mine. The miners, who rarely venture outdoors, can tell the weather is bad when they see a group of truckers-turned-tourists wandering through their tunnels.

When a storm calms, dump trucks pushing ten-foot high plows, graders and Cats set out to re-open the road. That can take seven hours, or longer if it was a particularly bad storm. Sometimes the road disappears and has to be rebuilt from scratch.

When building the ice road, Echo Bay uses a helicopter to steer the plows and graders in the right direction and to keep them in a straight line. The road is improved each year as curves are straightened and bumps on land crossings are ironed out.

The road was miserably rough in its first year, Klaus recalled. "You would be dropping in between rocks, getting stuck and tearing your truck apart. A lot of guys came up to work and they wouldn't even make one trip. They'd just sell their equipment and go home empty-handed. I just about felt like doing that too, but I decided to hang around a little bit longer and just take it easy. With more traffic over the road, I felt it had to get better. By March the road shaped up pretty good."

Echo Bay Mines spends up to $2 million a year developing and maintaining the road. But it saves $4 million using the road in place of air travel. About three and half million gallons of fuel and fourteen million pounds of supplies are hauled to the mine site every winter. The road contributes about $10 million to the Northwest Territories' economy each year and creates 150 seasonal jobs.

People from Yellowknife often drive the road out of curiosity. Native hunters and trappers — Dene from the Yellowknife area at the south end and Coppermine Inuit at the north end — use the road for easy access to game. During the road's early years, hunters would skin caribou in the middle of the road. They would leave behind the parts they do not use — the animals' intestines — which would freeze as hard as rock and become driving hazards. The problem was resolved after company officials spoke with the hunters, who agreed to skin their caribou off to the side. Echo Bay Mines does not have the authority to keep people off the road. It is built entirely on public land and so it cannot be considered a private drive.

Mining and oil companies have been building ice roads to gain access to isolated resources since the earliest days of northern development. Before the Lupin road, Echo Bay Mines used a winter route from Yellowknife to Port Radium on Great Bear Lake, until the mine there closed in 1982. The Port Radium road also served the Dene communities of Lac La Martre and Rae Lakes. The government of the Northwest Territories still opens that road each year. Once a community has a winter road, the people come to expect it. Even if the resource development ceases, public pressure forces the government to keep the road open.

Most communities in the western Northwest Territories are connected by the winter road and are otherwise accessible only by plane, snowmobile or boat. The territorial government spends about $2 million each year to build 1,219 kilometers of snow and ice roads. The winter routes are usually open for three months — January, February and March.

A person's first drive across ice can be frightening. "The first thing I thought," Klaus said, "was that it was okay if there was snow on top of the ice, but wherever I saw clear ice, it just looked like open water. It didn't take too long to get used to that. But then another bad thing was the overflows. You'd get cracks in the ice and you'd get water gushing out. You'd drive through it, the water would come up on your windshield and freeze. Then you wouldn't see a thing. That's kind of scary too until you get used to it."

The ice cracks after the weather changes from one extreme to another, either from warm to cold or from cold to warm. Once a truck driver pulled over to sleep and there was overnight flooding. His tires were frozen into the ice by the time he awoke. He ended up ripping his tire treads and tearing apart his drive shaft trying to get out.

Nevertheless, the journey across ice can just as often be tedious. "Unless you get into a storm or bad ice, you really don't have to keep your mind on your work that much. You're going fairly slow and you're just day dreaming away. You've got a lot of time to think, that's for sure," said Klaus.

Fox or wolverine sightings help break the monotony of the ice road. Klaus also has had to stop for herds of caribou migrating across his path. Flocks of ptarmigan — a type of northern grouse — will entertain him by flying alongside the truck for several minutes. The playful birds then take turns cutting sharply in front of the windshield, like children playing a game of chicken.

The feathered friends are not Fast Eddie's only company. In his rear-view mirror he can see his driving partner in the distance. Trucks have been required to travel in pairs ever since one broke down when the temperature was -40 degrees and the driver froze his hands while making repairs.

Klaus and his partner are constantly talking to each other over their CB radios. They are often plotting practical jokes and college-type pranks to play on other drivers. On one occasion a trucker was bragging over his CB about how good his radio was on his new Mack. Klaus's partner replied that the radio in Fast Eddie's old '82 Ford LTL 9000 could quite clearly pick up CFCW, a country and western station from Camrose, Alberta, that is a favourite of truckers. The boastful Mack driver bet that it was impossible. Klaus had a cassette recording of the station. He slid it into his tape deck and turned on his CB. The other driver listened in disbelief. "He was really upset that I could get Camrose, but he couldn't," Klaus said. "Anytime you can play a little trick like that, you do it."

If the road is closed and the drivers are stuck at a camp, there will be much discussion and debate about anything and everything, including the standings in their friendly competition of who will make the most trips to Lupin this year. It is not difficult to figure out who is in the lead and why.

"I would be in there talking to the guys, keeping them all relaxed and everything, while my partner was out watching," said Fast Eddie. "The minute he had the word that the road was open, he'd just come and give me a nod — he didn't have to say anything — and we were gone.

"Near the end of the season, the others were getting wise, they were catching on to some of our tricks. There was one guy who got ahead of me running out the door and he fell going down the steps. I never slowed down. I trampled right over top of him and I was in my truck and we were gone." Klaus prefers northern trucking to the impersonal highway system of southern Canada. "In the South, you've got more people to deal with. Here you kind of do what you want to do. You're more free. There are no traffic laws on the ice. You don't have weight limits and if you have big loads, you don't have to have pilot cars. You don't have to worry about lights or having flags. You have your own little laws on the ice. You help each other out."

Alone on the barren lands, Klaus often muses about going home. "When you come home, you can usually expect two or three months where you're not really doing anything. You're hanging around downtown, going to auction sales, just more or less killing the time. You've got your hockey playoffs at night, but during the day, you're out drinking coffee. I keep myself busy that way — not physically, but with my mind. Sometimes there are all kinds of work I want to do around the house, but this or that guy comes by and talks a little bit. I'm busy all day, but I never do anything. The wife gets upset with me sometimes. She figures all I ever do is talk, but sometimes you don't see these people too often and they always want to know how your winter's work went..."

Klaus' summer work begins soon enough. By June he is back in his truck hauling gravel from pits to be spread on the North's year-round roads. In the fall he cuts and sells firewood, "just to keep myself busy," he said. "A guy can't lay around too much or he'll get lazy and then he won't feel like doing anything."

When winter returns Klaus is back on that familiar road with no street signs and very little on-coming traffic. There may be ninety trucks on the Lupin ice road at any one time, "but you would never know it," he said. "Scattered out over 400 miles, I guess they're out there some place."

The Arctic ice road is no place for the standard "no riders" rule. "Up here it's very easy to get into trouble. You never leave anybody stranded," Klaus said. "Not only truckers, but if you see hunters, anybody who is stranded, you get them to the nearest camp."

Klaus drives and lives by a philosophy preached to him by a man he once drove for early in his northern trucking career. His former boss, Klaus said, "wanted his trucks to go up and down the road as fast as they could go, but he wanted us to be gentlemen about it."

PART IV
MODERN LIVES

TOM JEYACHANDRAN: THE FLYING DOCTOR

When he was a medical doctor in India, Tom Jeyachandran, a cosmopolitan man who had done post graduate work in England, read stories of romance and adventure set in the Canadian Arctic. These stories had an effect — he decided that he wanted to work among the Inuit.

Not knowing whom to approach or where to write for such a job, he went to Canada to find out. From England, he moved on to Montreal, where he worked for a year before discovering that the federal Department of Health and Welfare hired doctors for the North. He went to apply and told the woman who interviewed him that he was interested only in a job in the North.

"Why on earth do you want to go there?" she asked.

"I'm just curious," Jeyachandran replied.

"I think you're crazy, but you can have the job."

The government assigned the Tamil doctor to Fort Rae. Not surprisingly, he had never heard of the place. He took out some library books about the North and learned that not a single Inuit lived in Fort Rae. It is a community of about 1,500 Dene Indians, on the north shore of Great Slave Lake.

Jeyachandran and his wife, Anne, and their first two (of an eventual five) children drove to Fort Rae in 1967 in a beat-up old Volkswagon van with the steering on the right-hand side, which they had brought to Canada from England. They stopped in Edmonton for an "orientation," but still nobody knew much about the Northwest Territories. Most certainly nobody mentioned that Jeyachandran would have to go to the toilet in a pail called a "honey bucket." But since he came from India, "it was not a big surprise or handicap."

He arrived in Fort Rae and inspected the local hospital. It was a Catholic mission hospital, run by the Grey Nuns. He could not understand why the building faced the lake. People had to use the back door to go in and out. "I debated this and later on I found out it was because there was no road and all the traffic (airplanes, snowmobiles and dog teams) was by the lake."

Fort Rae, or "Rae" as it is just as often called, is located on a peninsula. Its people are the Dogrib tribe of the Dene nation. They live now, as they did over two decades ago when Jeyachandran first arrived there, in over-crowded log houses many of which are heated by wood. Many Dogrib people hunt and fish for their livelihood and cook meat over open fires, or smoke it in teepee-shaped smoke houses. They smoke a lot of cigarettes. They live in conditions ideal for respiratory diseases, notably tuberculosis. Aboriginal people have yet to build up a resistance to tuberculosis, a disease brought to North America by the early European explorers. When, after a long absence, Jeyachandran returned to Fort Rae in 1983, he found TB still well entrenched. Over a dozen cases of tuberculosis are treated every year in the community. That is less than the 1960s average of over seventy cases a year, "but doctors can't take credit," Jeyachandran said. "The living conditions improved and there were fewer diseases. I think more and more money should be spent on better housing."

Jeyachandran can take credit, however, for keeping tuberculosis patients at home. When he first came to Rae, Northerners with the disease were sent to sanatoriums in southern Canada. When they returned north perhaps ten years later, they no longer knew their own families. And even if they did, they would not have been able to communicate because they had lost their native language.

"I thought sending people away was backwards," Jeyachandran said. "I was willing to treat them here because I had done it before. Ottawa wasn't willing to let me do it at first, but the northern medical unit really pushed."

Even then, people with tuberculosis were treated at the local hospital for several years. Now they are treated as outpatients. They take their drugs, several times a week for a minimum of nine months, at home.

In Fort Rae, Jeyachandran is called "Doctor Tom" or just "Doc," a nickname often spoken in a jocular tone. He is a large man with a thick, grey beard who eats a lot of junk food, particularly tortilla chips. And he is always laughing. The people he works among, the Dogrib, also have a good sense of humour. Once Jeyachandran spoke to parents about some head lice that he had found rampant at the school. Somebody said something in Dogrib and everyone laughed. When the doctor asked for a translation, he was told that he was finding lice because he got paid to find lice. Jeyachandran responded that, if that was the case, he would be a millionaire soon. Everyone laughed again.

Yet Jeyachandran missed a lot of the Dogrib humour, and even a real sense of belonging, by not speaking the local language. "I did make an effort to study Dogrib, but it's such a complicated language you would have to do immersion study for two years. I'm too old for that," he said when he was fifty-nine years old.

The training of medical interpreters in the North is a recent phenomenon, but even now many medical terms do not translate into the aboriginal languages. "You really don't know what they are interpreting or whether or not they are getting the message across. Sometimes you get in some pretty funny situations when you are talking about different parts of the body."

After eighteen months in Fort Rae, Jeyachandran "still wanted to go further north and work with the Eskimo." He took a posting in Cambridge Bay, an Inuit community in the central Arctic. He found the Inuit quite different from the Dene. "With the Indians, their aggression and anger comes out, so you know exactly what's going on. With the Inuit, you don't know. They don't say a lot, so it's difficult to figure out the medical problem."

Many Inuit still lived on the land, which made for some difficult emergency medical evacuations, commonly referred to as "medevacs." Once Jeyachandran set out to pick up a patient and the plane landed at the wrong hunting camp. It was about forty degrees below zero, so some Inuit hunters gave the doctor a pair of caribou skin pants and took him by snowmobile to the right camp. They pulled the patient back on a toboggan and put him and Jeyachandran on the plane, which flew back to Cambridge Bay.

The Inuit knew Jeyachandran as the "flying doctor." He tried to visit each hunting camp once a month. "We used to chug along in a single engine Otter and it would take all day to reach some of these places, so we would have to do a clinic in the middle of the night."

Being the only doctor in the region, he also held medical clinics in other central Arctic communities. They too were usually in the evening because that was when space was available. In the settlement of Holman, clinics were held in a school room. The doctor would push together the child-size desks and have his patients lie on them for examination. Eventually, a small nursing station was built at the edge of Holman's airstrip. "I was dropped off right at the gate. I used to get out of the plane and walk straight into the nursing cabin to do a clinic."

After a year in the central Arctic, Jeyachandran and his family said, "Okay, we've seen the North and we're not coming back."

"You'll be back," their friends told them.

As he was about to leave Cambridge Bay, several doctors at the Yellowknife hospital were suspended and Jeyachandran was asked to fill in until new ones were hired. He was the only doctor in Yellowknife for several weeks, at a time when the city's population was soaring.

It was the first time Jeyachandran bailed the northern Canadian medical establishment out of trouble. It would not be the last.

The first time Jeyachandran left the North, in 1969, he decided that he would also leave medicine. He went back to India to try his hand at farming, but after ten months he was broke. He applied for a doctor's job at the foothills of the Himalayas in Bhutan, and he also wrote back to Canada.

The reply from Canada came quickly. Needing the money, he immediately accepted a job in the North. Then came an offer from Bhutan. "Oh well, that's the way it goes," he said.

He was to return to Fort Rae, but enroute the administrative director for the Keewatin, based in Churchill, Manitoba, had a heart attack. Jeyachandran agreed to fill the suddenly vacant position.

Then the Department of Health and Welfare asked him to be the administrator in the Yukon. "They told me there were a lot of political problems there. I said that I didn't mind, I'd try anything once."

He arrived in Whitehorse to discover that the hospital had lost its accreditation because of failing to meet a set of national standards. He got it back within a year, but not until after dealing with in-fighting between two factions of doctors, conflicts between the federal and Yukon governments over which should provide health care services, and an Alaska newspaper report about an outbreak of food poisoning that had started in the Yukon. Investigation proved the newspaper correct — a Yukon hotel's sewage was leaking into its drinking water.

In 1973, Tom and Anne Jeyachandran packed their five children, aged eighteen months to ten years, in a new Volkswagon van and left Whitehorse for South America. The doctor picked up work — four to six months at a time, long enough for the children to get some schooling — along the way, at a British hospital in Belize, an Anglican missionary hospital in Columbia, an American evangelical mission in Ecuador, and a Catholic mission in Peru.

Jeyachandran thought that he finally had an opportunity to use his expertise in tropical medicine training which he received during his years of study in England. But he learned differently. During the last year of his South American sojourn, he walked with a preacher deep into the Ecuadorian jungle through miles of mud to reach a village of the Auca tribe, which came into contact with western civilization only in the late 1950s. Coca-Cola had arrived there first. Jeyachandran found that he had to pull teeth rather than practise tropical medicine.

Since the Catholic missionary hospital in Peru ran on faith rather than money, the Jeyachandran family was soon broke again. With their van about to blow its second engine — the first went on a mountain in Colombia — they looked for a cheap ticket to Europe, where they could stay with Anne's parents. They found a three-and-a-half week voyage on a Polish freighter.

There was a telegram from Ottawa awaiting Jeyachandran in London. An administrator was needed in Inuvik, N.W.T. "Sure," he told the Health and Welfare officials, "but what's the problem? You don't just go looking around the world for a zone director in Inuvik."

There was a big problem. A year earlier, a surgeon had arrived in Inuvik from Italy, via Africa and Chicago. He was hired to work at the local hospital and started living with a nurse. One day, his wife, whom he had left in Italy, came north, and the nurse quickly moved out. But Inuvik is a small town and before long the wife found out about her husband's girlfriend. The wife returned to Europe and gave her husband's whereabouts to Interpol, which was looking for him for fraud. Interpol contacted the RCMP, who then discovered that he had never been a doctor at all and he had been performing operations and prescribing medicine without any formal training.

"He was the best doctor I ever had," said the Mountie who arrested him.

"Obviously he was a charismatic figure. People thought he did a hell of a good job," Jeyachandran commented. "To be a good doctor, you have to be kind and have a rapport with people. You can kill them, they'll still say you're a great doctor."

Jeyachandran spent a year in Inuvik, restoring the hospital's reputation and obtaining its full national accreditation. He did not like the job, however, because by the mid 1970s administration involved too much paper work. When he had run the medical services in the Keewatin and Yukon, "administration was common sense, none of this following rules and regulations. If you broke a rule, so what. Nobody was bothered by it."

He decided to try farming again, this time near Fort St. John, British Columbia. Again, it did not work out. He was registered to practise medicine in Nova Scotia, and so he moved there and opened a private clinic in a sleepy fishing village of 800, mostly elderly, people. "It was an easy practice. We made enough to live on. Unfortunately I was not ready to have a retired life," he said.

He and his wife decided they had had enough of Canada and found work in rural Brunei, in southeast Asia. Their children finished school there and the oldest two returned to Canada for university. "We decided we might as well go back to Canada to be near the kids. So this time we wrote Ottawa for a job." He would only go north, of course. He was made the administrator for the Mackenzie region, based in Yellowknife. As in Inuvik, the job was too top-heavy. He stuck with it for two years, during which time the doctor's position in Fort Rae came open. "It came under my authority, so I kept it vacant," he said. He hired himself in 1984 and returned to the job he had started almost two decades earlier. This time, he stayed in Fort Rae for four years, and then left to work overseas as a doctor at Canadian embassies.

The job in Rae was easier the second time around. The old mission hospital was closed and patients were sent 100 kilometers away to the modern Yellowknife hospital. People were getting better treatment, Jeyachandran said, but practising medicine was not as exciting as when the facilities were limited, far away or not available. Before, people brought Doctor Tom their dogs to stitch up. Now, snowmobiles had replaced dog teams, and he stitched up people who were hurt in snowmobiling accidents. He was no longer a frontier doctor. "Now it's like working anywhere else in Canada."

In the North, there has been much talk about having native people take more responsibility for their own health care. There is the occasional push to train native nurses, but it certainly is not happening overnight. "There is this prevailing thought that if you go out and train to be a nurse, you should come back to your own community to work. That is nonsense," Jeyachandran said. "The demand on that poor girl would be so much, she would go crazy. The same people would ask me why didn't I go work in India."

Other ideas for native involvement in medicine have been "poo-pooed and thrown out," he said. "Local people can be trained to do a specific job. We need someone who can do just TB work, or someone trained to do pre-natal work. But people in this country are worried about legal things. In so-called under-developed countries, they can go ahead and do it."

Many northern natives are rediscovering traditional forms of medicine. These range from applying spruce gum to frostbite and open cuts, to spiritual healing. A Dogrib woman once gave Jeyachandran a root of a plant, which was used to cure headaches. He carried it in his doctor's bag and would prescribe it on occasion. Coming from India, where there are also alternative medicines, Jeyachandran encouraged the use of traditional Dene medicines. Through the local friendship centre, he arranged for a Cree medicine man from Alberta to give a workshop in Fort Rae, as there are so few Dene practitioners left.

"I always ask the people here why they want to take so many pills when I'm sure they have their local herbs," he said. "People are confused to a certain extent. Like anybody, they want to get the best of both worlds. So they use the traditional medicine and then they come to me to get some pills, just to be sure. I've seen it here, I've seen it in Guatemala where they pray and do their traditional rituals and then they go to church. In India, that's very common. They go to everything — church, temple and mosque — to get the blessing of every god."

The Dogrib people have told Jeyachandran more and more about their traditional beliefs and curses as they have come to know and respect him over the years. "Many civilizations have what you might call their superstitions," he said. "But unless they know you intimately, they won't tell you anything, because they think you're going to laugh at them."

The people of Fort Rae know Doctor Tom intimately because he is a genuine person. He is a doctor who has always, and who will always, make house calls. He is a doctor whose fondest memories of Fort Rae, of the North, of around the world, are about "working with the people." Jeyachandran has a strong conviction that "people are the same everywhere you go." He should know.

T. DAVID MARSHALL: THE HIGHEST JUDGE

T. David Marshall is a medical doctor, a university professor, a published author, an airplane pilot, a militiaman, and an honorary chief of the Six Nations Indian reserve. Oh yes, and his full-time job is as a Supreme Court judge.

Once the only practising doctor and lawyer in Canada, in 1982 Marshall left his various clinics in southwestern Ontario to become one of only two high court judges in the Northwest Territories. "I call it the highest judicial appointment in Canada," he said. "Geographically it's the highest."

It helps to have a sense of humour to be a judge in the North. "If you were a nervous edgy type, you would go nuts," Marshall said.

Example? "Well, I'm sitting in a town hall, which also serves as the court room in this community, and I've just sentenced a young aboriginal man to a year in jail for assault. He's a tough, strong guy with big muscles. I go back into what is somebody's office. I've got my shirt half off. I've got my gown off. The clerk comes in with the accused, and she says, 'My Lord, this fellow won't sign the probation report.' I said, 'I can't talk to him without his lawyer here.' Before I could say 'jackrabbit,' she's out the door to get his lawyer. I'm standing here with my clothes half off alone with the guy who I just sentenced to jail. In Ontario of course, he'd have a police officer with him. But up here, the Mounties know the guy, they know what he's like. They just let him roam around.

"In the South, judges are chauffeur-driven in black limousines. They're taken to and from everything with security guards. We don't have security guards here. I even have my name down where I park my car. I feel perfectly safe on the street, but I don't go into the bars because I would inevitably run into somebody who was half-cut whom I had sentenced. But that's about the only limitation on my lifestyle."

Marshall's lifestyle consists of trying and doing anything imaginable. His curriculum vitae reads like a best-seller.

He graduated from the University of Toronto medical school in 1963 and practised medicine while attending Osgoode Hall law school. Then he worked part time as a lawyer and part time as a doctor at firms and clinics in and around his home town of Cayuga, Ontario. He ran a medical clinic and did legal work at the nearby Six Nations Indian reserve, where he was made an honorary chief. Even as a judge, Marshall does rounds at the Yellowknife hospital every Thursday, and he is a member of the Northwest Territories Medical Association. "I've got to be the only judge in the world who carries medical malpractice insurance," he said.

A specialist on the relationship between law and medicine, he has written four books *The Canadian Law of Inquests*, *The Physician and Canadian Law*, *Patients' Rights*, and *The Medical Law Handbook* and numerous articles for legal and medical journals. He has given lectures and speeches around the world. He is the chairman of a national committee on ethics in medical research, and the founding chairman of the Northwest Territories Law Reform Committee. In 1988, he was hired to run the Ottawa-based Canadian Judicial Centre, a new organization to educate judges at all levels across the country. He would at the same time, however, keep his judgeship in the North.

The military is his hobby. He has been involved in the armed forces reserves since high school, and he served a summer in Germany as the doctor for the Canadian forces stationed there. Marshall has also been the medical officer for the military's Northern Region headquarters in Yellowknife.

A dabbling in politics included a term as president of the southern Ontario Young Conservatives while at university, but he liked Pierre Trudeau and ended up running for the Liberals in his home town during the federal elections of 1972 and 1974. He was beaten soundly both times.

After his disastrous attempt at a political career, Marshall went back to school, to Oxford University, for over a year. He returned to Canada to teach criminal law at the University of Windsor and medicine at McMaster University, and also travelled around Ontario as a provincial coroner. A holder of a pilot's licence since the age of fifteen, Marshall commuted to his various worksites in his single-engine Beech Baron.

It was his private aircraft that first brought him to the Arctic in 1981. He flew to Baffin Island and spent the summer working as a travelling medical doctor, flying from one Inuit community to another. His time on Baffin and his work with native people at the Six Nations reserve "probably helped" him land the appointment to the Northwest Territories bench when he was forty-two years old, young for a high court judge. "It was fortunate I had shown some interest in native people," he said.

In court, Marshall is known to give stiff sentences for sexual assault and child abuse, but soft ones for most other crimes. Many northern judges are considered "too lenient" and cynics say that if you plan to kill somebody, it is best to do it in the Northwest Territories.

"In the North, it's hard to be tough enough," Marshall said. "The public wants you to give tough sentences. It's fine to say that, but I can remember one of my very early cases. A chap was accused of something and his mother was sitting in the court room. They point her out to me. She was about eighty years old. He brought in his neighbours who said that when it snowed, he was the first guy to shovel the snow. If anybody's car broke down, he was the first guy to fix it. What do you do with a guy like that? You really don't feel inclined to throw the book at him with his elderly mother sitting there and his wife sitting there and his children sitting there."

The Northwest Territories has the highest crime rate in Canada, the highest rate of violent crime and the highest percentage of its people in jail. Yet Marshall insisted that "we don't have criminals up here.

"We have a problem with crime, but we don't have a problem with criminality. Our crime may be violent, but it is simple and straightforward. I've never had a conspiracy case up here. I don't think people even know what conspiracy is around here. We don't have people who have been doctoring ten thousand documents that the court has to go through. We don't have complex fraud cases. We don't get corporations that are beating this guy or beating the government. We don't have indigenous organized crime. We don't have indigenous drug dealers. We don't have anything that's not fueled by a night's drinking or a big party."

Crimes in the North are almost always alcohol-related. The alcohol problem, Marshall claimed, is related to many things: isolation, winter darkness, a rapidly changing society, "and a number of other things which I'm sure we don't understand."

When handing down a sentence, a white judge from Ontario cannot always know how much weight cultural differences should carry. Marshall once heard a case in a small Dene community involving a battered wife. The defence submission was that wife beating was considered acceptable, based on aboriginal culture. The female defence lawyer called chiefs and elders from nearby communities to testify what the practice was if a wife "misbehaved." The first chief said it was their custom to beat her. The next chief said the same thing. And the accused admitted he beat his wife, but he did it because it was part of his culture.

Then, from the back of the full court room, a native woman yelled out: "Bullshit!"

With changing values in the North, "who knows what the native custom is, or was, or what they think now," Marshall said.

Marshall has taken language lessons in Inuktitut and Dogrib, one of the five Dene languages, to help him better understand northern cultures. "Nobody expects the judge to understand a word of the native language. When you do pick something up and when you speak a few words, people just about swallow their teeth because they're so shocked." Marshall feels strongly about the need for judges to have northern experience. "Appeal judges from the South who sometimes come up here don't appreciate the realities of the North," he said.

When an Inuit hunter returns home from a hunt, he will put his caribou or musk ox meat into an unlocked community freezer and everyone in town helps themselves. The concept of stealing is foreign to the native people whose culture is based on sharing. Under the Canadian law, break and enter is one of the most serious crimes and a person can receive life imprisonment for it. "Here someone going into another native person's house and helping themselves to the caribou is no crime at all," Marshall said. "There's no doubt in my mind that entering a dwelling house at night in the Arctic is considered perfectly all right under all circumstances."

Much of the Northwest Territories' population is Inuit and Dene — people who live in small, isolated communities and speak only one of the Northwest Territories' seven aboriginal languages, each with numerous dialects. There have been situations where an arrested person is told he has the right to counsel, but he thinks the police are talking about the local town council. "How do you offer a guy the right to counsel anyway when there is no lawyer within 700 miles? Realistically, what sort of a right is it? The law is different up here," Marshall said.

Many Northerners' only impression of the law is what they see during the irregular and occasional visits of a court party. They see everyone — the judge, defence lawyers, Crown prosecutor, clerk, sheriff and court reporter — arrive together on a DC-3, conduct their business and leave together a few hours later.

"Consider this," Marshall said. "Your son is charged with a crime. The court comes to town and he is tried in a language you don't understand at all. At the end of the court case, they clamp the handcuffs on him and they take him away for five years. Would you as a Canadian citizen feel that you had been fairly dealt with? You would be aghast."

Based on the work of Marshall's Law Reform Committee, the Northwest Territories government passed a bill in 1986 to allow unilingual native jurors, which will make the Northwest Territories the only jurisdiction in Canada where a person who does not speak English or French can serve on a jury. Two years later, the bill had yet to be proclaimed as law because there were still some "administrative problems." Native language dictionaries for each of the Northwest Territories' seven aboriginal languages were required and court interpreters had to be trained. There also was the sticky question of how jurors who spoke different languages would communicate. The government would have to decide if interpreters would be let into the sacred grounds of the juror room.

Yet Marshall emphasized that such laws are part of the overall solution, "a careful, humane application of the law, with legal education being fundamentally important."

He also argued that public education is an important reason to continue the legendary practice of the northern circuit court. Northern courts have held trials in school gymnasiums and community halls in remote aboriginal settlements since the 1950s. Before then, without exception, court was held in Yellowknife or southern Canada. The Northwest Territories government now spends half a million dollars a year to transport, feed and accommodate travelling parties of the Supreme Court and the lower Territorial Court.

Just as he is the boss of the court room, the judge is in charge of the airplane on which the court party flies. Marshall has been known to bump defence lawyers from a full plane after a trial, in favour of guests and journalists travelling with the court party. Marshall often has journalists or writers or film crews — his unofficial biographers — on board the court's aircraft. To delight the scribes, he may even jump into the cockpit and fly the airplane himself. Members of the bar and court say Marshall has an inflated ego, but then, many add, so do all good judges and lawyers.

Once a prosecuting lawyer asked Marshall if a drunken star witness could be locked up for the night so he could take the stand the next day in a sober state. The judge decided to let him go.

"You're making a mistake. That guy will be drunk tomorrow and he won't be back," the clerk whispered to Marshall as they were leaving the court room.

"That's why I'm the judge and you're the clerk," Marshall responded.

There are only two justices of the Northwest Territories Supreme Court — Marshall and Mark deWeerdt. DeWeerdt is senior in years on the bench, but there is no formal "chief justice" position. The two judges split up the cases between themselves. Their styles contrast considerably. Marshall is public and rhetorical; DeWeerdt is more restrained and keeps a lower public profile. Yet they have argued only once in five years, Marshall said. "We just got on each other's nerves. You get bushed up here. Around January and February you almost reach a pathological stage; you really wonder if you should be making judgements." High court judges in the North have a profound impact on the development of the law. Since the Northwest Territories court was just born in 1955, their decisions are not bound by hundreds of years of precedent-setting cases. "In Ontario or Quebec you might have forty or fifty judges doing what we're doing, and any issue that you want to think of has already been handled and rehandled several times," Marshall said. "Up in the North, we're getting new issues all the time and they've never been dealt with before. We have the benefit of looking to see how they messed it up in Quebec, what a good job they did in Ontario, how they did it in Saskatchewan. We can be innovative here where you can't anywhere else. We have a tremendous latitude and freedom in interpreting the law."

The federal Criminal Code provides for a smaller jury in the northern territories, in recognition of the smaller, widely scattered population. A northern native challenged the six-person jury in 1985 and Justice deWeerdt found it discriminatory under the Charter of Rights and Freedoms in that other Canadians had the right to a twelve-person jury. So the six-person jury was thrown out.

In a case before Justice Marshall a year later, another native person argued that he had a right to a six-person jury. Twelve impartial jurors could not be found in his tiny home town, and the Crown prosecutor wanted to move the trial to another community. The accused claimed that he was being deprived of a trial by his peers. Marshall, noting the Criminal Code said one thing and the Charter allowed for another, ruled that an accused person in the Northwest Territories had the option of being tried by either a six-member or a twelve-member jury.

Marshall hears only about eighty cases a year, most of them relating to the Charter of Rights and Freedoms, which became part of the Canadian Constitution in 1982. As Northerners learn more about the law that is so foreign to their way of life and launch more challenges under the Charter, the legal system could change drastically.

A person living in a small settlement, where the closest lawyer is hundreds of miles away, has yet to bring a challenge under the Charter's right-to-counsel clause. Nobody has used the Charter's provision for freedom of religion to push for the teaching of traditional native religious practices in the schools. The guarantee to life, liberty and security has not been used against animal rights groups or icebreaking ships that threaten the Inuit's traditional way of life. Police searches without a warrant in communities where there is prohibition of alcohol have not faced the section of the Charter dealing with unreasonable search and seizure. Nobody from southern Canada has applied the Charter's mobility rights to the Northwest Territories government's policy of giving preference to Northerners when awarding jobs and contracts.

The list goes on. A challenge under any one of these Charter provisions could affect everyday life in the North.

"There are so many interesting cases here," said the man who will decide many of them. "There are more personal challenges here than I could have imagined. There are more challenges here than you can meet."

EDNA ELIAS: CHALLENGING TRADITIONAL ATTITUDES

Women in the Inuit community of Coppermine feared men who were walking the streets while awaiting trials for sexual assault. There was thus absolute outrage in July 1985, when the chief judge of the territorial court said that the local Mounties had "gone crazy" for sending an accused to Yellowknife for a hearing to determine if he should be held in custody. Since he had had only two other "Mickey Mouse" assaults, said the judge, "I'm not going to keep this guy in custody, my golly. Why in the name of the devil has he been arrested and sent down here and taken up our time and the taxpayers money?"

Many local people thought that the comments undermined efforts to correct one of the North's most serious social problems. They said that women would remain silent about beatings to avoid ridicule while the culprit would believe that what he did was petty. They turned to Edna Elias for help. She was more than the town's mayor; she was its guidance counsellor, mediator, lobbyist and leader.

A public meeting was called and 200 people signed a petition to the Northwest Territories government which stated: "We are displeased and angry with the justice system and decisions of certain judges that allow offenders charged with sexual assault involving violence back into our communities pending trials."

Elias asked other communities for support and nearby Cambridge Bay responded with a petition for the judge's removal from the bench. For the first time, the Northwest Territories Judicial Council, headed by the senior justice of the Supreme Court, reviewed the performance of a lower court judge. While it concluded that the judge's comments should not have been made from the bench, it did not criticize the decision he had handed down. Yet the public outcry shook the usually secure legal community. Elias observed about six months after the incident that "everyone is being more careful of the comments they make in public office, whether they're sitting on the bench or are out somewhere in the evening." She was also convinced that from this point on, "people who were charged were not running around in the communities as free as a bird."

Elias had always been working to make Coppermine a better community for her fellow Inuit, even when she sat on the hamlet council as a teenager in the 1970s. Then she was a most valuable member of the council's recreation committee because she was good at raising money and organizing events. To hold spring carnivals, Christmas games or to buy equipment, funds were raised through weekly movie nights. "We got out the old popcorn maker and bagged popcorn the night before, and we would rent these old spaghetti westerns or horror movies from Edmonton and the community hall was packed."

But the introduction of television to Coppermine in 1974 proved to be a force that even Elias could not overcome. Television did more than ruin the community's main fund raising source; "it really destroyed all social life," she said. "You wouldn't see kids playing out on the street or people out for a walk after supper. Everybody was glued to the tube."

People reappeared after a year or so, when the novelty of television started to wear, but the movie nights were never the same. By that time bingo had become the latest rage across the North, and some hamlets had to pass by-laws to limit the number of games held each week because there was concern about people spending all their money on bingo cards rather than on food for their children. However, said Elias, bingo never got "out of control" in Coppermine, where games are held only one night a week.

Elias said that her leadership and organizational skills must have come from her mother. Seven of her mother's eleven children were girls, so by numbers alone, the women of the family were not dominated by the men. "It's unusual in the Inuit tradition that women should be so vocal and in the forefront," Elias said. "I think there are times when I have embarrassed my husband or the way I have approached something may not seem right, but it works out for the benefit of the people."

Changing attitudes has not been easy for Inuit men, Elias said. "There are still a lot of thick skulls. I'd be afraid too if the other sex was going to start running the world after being dominated for so long."

Elias was a classroom assistant in Coppermine for six years before enrolling at the teacher's college at Fort Smith in 1978. After teaching in another Inuit community, she returned to Coppermine in 1982. The following year, when she was twenty-nine years old and working as a teacher at the local school, she was elected mayor of Coppermine. She finished the school year trying to do both jobs, but decided she had to quit one to do the other well. She chose to stop teaching because of a quarrel with the principal, who would not let her instruct an Inuktitut language course. "I was so appalled and I couldn't understand the reasoning for it," she said.

The school principal also sat on the hamlet council, as did a businessman, trapper, seamstress and housewife. The group argued hard and long; meetings often lasted well past midnight. As mayor, Elias was supposed to keep order. "Sometimes I'd walk into a meeting and tell myself that I wasn't going to let this get out of hand, or that I wasn't going to let one guy blab too long, but then I'd get so into it myself that I didn't want to cut them off."

Once, in 1985, the councillors forced Elias to resign after they hired her husband, Fred, as the hamlet's secretary-manager. Since the mayor and secretary-manager were the signing authorities for hamlet cheques, the councillors thought that there could be a potential conflict of interest. She stepped down "with a little bit of regret" and told the councillors she would run again in the next election, which she easily won. "I was confident I'd get back in. I'd show them that people could trust us."

Unlike the secretary-manager, the mayor's job in Coppermine, home to about 900 people, is not considered full-time work. Rather than a salary, she received an honourarium for each meeting she attended. Yet Elias dedicated each afternoon to the task, which, in Coppermine, included counselling people looking for a job, needing help with their income tax returns or complaining about the government. And she would speak with the media, under certain conditions. "I used to give the CBC heck when they called me at nine o'clock in the morning and say, 'Edna, can we talk to you about this or that?'. I'd tell them that the mornings are my own time, call me back in the afternoon."

The media inquiries often concerned the Coppermine post office, which was more or less a run-down shack. It did not have a mail box, so people had to wait until it opened to post a letter. And by then there were usually forty others standing in line to send letters, buy stamps, pick up mail (as there was no home delivery or site boxes), or purchase money orders (an important function of the post office in communities where there are no banks). There was only one employee, so the office closed while she sorted the mail. In 1984, the hamlet council launched a petition calling for improved service. This one was also signed by 200 people, which prompted the Yellowknife postmaster to fly to Coppermine to meet with the council. He acknowledged that the building was a fire trap: "It is so small, they have to pile up the mail next to the furnace and you can't even get in or out the back door." But there was nothing he could do about it because the building belonged to the Department of Public Works. "Every year DPW comes up, looks at it and goes back," said one councillor. "Then they come back the next year and say 'yep, it's worse than it was last year,' and leave again."

The postmaster suggested that the hamlet run the postal service under contract. The council tried to lease Canada Post space, but it was offered only $2,000 a year, which would not even cover heating costs. "What a lost battle that one was," Elias said four years later. "They change the sign maybe once every two years, but it's still the same building."

The building in which people in Coppermine do take pride is the recreation complex, which includes a gymnasium and hockey arena. It was constructed with local volunteer labour, government grants and donations from businesses and the community as a whole. The grants from government were the smallest source of revenue — and that suited the community just fine. "We didn't want the government constructing some big space-aged building with domed windows that wouldn't meet our needs," Elias said.

Elias was also behind a scheme to renovate some old Ministry of Transport barracks for use as a combined shelter for battered women and group home for young offenders. But the government decided that the two groups could not be housed under one roof. "They said you can't have kids seeing these battered women, some of whom might be under the influence of alcohol and that's against regulations and all that crap," she said.

The building became a group home, but Coppermine never did get a women's shelter.

Since most family violence in northern communities is preceded by a night of heavy drinking, local women supported the setting of limits on the amount of alcohol brought into the community. Coppermine voters rejected liquor controls in plebiscites in 1983 and 1985, but such controls were eventually put in place after a third plebiscite in 1987.

By then, Elias had resigned as mayor and moved to Yellowknife to work for the Northwest Territories government. She was hired to head the native language bureau, which included forty-two Inuit and Dene translators. She was offered the position after co-chairing a six-person task force on the state of aboriginal languages in the North. After three months of emotional public hearings in twenty-four northern communities, the task force recommended that Northerners be given the right to receive government services in native languages, which would require interpreters at hospitals and nursing stations and during court proceedings. It further recommended the development of native language school books and curriculum so children could receive a bilingual education. To make it all possible, there had to be specialized training for interpreters and teachers, language courses for government managers, and media and library materials in native languages.

In its report, printed in seven languages, the task force envisioned a bilingual northern society where all people — native and white — spoke English and an aboriginal language. But after living in Yellowknife and working in the English-dominated bureaucracy, Elias realized just how difficult it will be to achieve the ideal. "I noticed that since I moved here, I started stuttering and stumbling over words when speaking my own dialect. Here, you can very easily forget you have your own language. You can understand how quickly the kids forget it."

She had been on the job for a couple of months when government leader Nick Sibbeston, in a public speech about daycare policy, said that he thought women should stay at home and raise their children. Elias told the press that she thought Sibbeston had a chauvinistic attitude. She was speaking in her capacity as president of the Northwest Territories Advisory Council on the Status of Women, a group that advises and lobbies the territorial government on women's and social issues, to which Elias was appointed in 1985. She thought nothing of her comments until she travelled the next day on government business to Fort Smith, where other bureaucrats told her that they were surprised she still had a job.

"I was a little bit nervous after that," Elias said. "I thought that maybe when I got back to Yellowknife there'd be a memo on my desk calling me up to the government leader's office."

The deputy minister of her department had already been hinting that she step down from the women's council. When she returned from Fort Smith, she said that she would resign as president, but not as a member of the council. The government gave its approval to this arrangement.

Partially because she was not comfortable with government gag orders and red tape, and partially because she did not want her or her two children to lose Inuktitut, which gave them "a sense of identity," Elias quit the civil service in 1988 and moved back to Coppermine.

She wanted to do "something different," but she was feeling pressure to run again for mayor even before she returned. "I don't know how people have a personal desire to be a politician," said Elias, "but I'll run if people want me to run."

TIGER

MARGARET THRASHER: TOWN DRUNK

Drinking mouthwash helps Margaret Thrasher get rid of the taste of her morning hang-over. At the same time, the alcohol content of most mouthwashes gives her an early start on yet another day of getting drunk.

At noon, when the Yellowknife liquor store opens, she and other local street people pool their money and buy a bottle of wine or 74 Canadian Sherry. They form a circle in a back alley and pass around the bottle. Thrasher prefers to drink outdoors, even on the coldest winter day, because she believes that the booze will sweat away if she is inside.

Somebody might accidentally buy a bottle with a cork. Under such complicated circumstances, Thrasher will take the bottle to one of the many dining lounges from which she has been blacklisted, and ask to borrow a corkscrew.

"I don't care where you open it, just don't let me see you do it," a bartender once told her.

It was uncorked, sort of, in the doorway into the lounge. After breaking off the bottle neck, Thrasher poured the wine into an empty bottle that she dug out of a garbage can.

Even though she goes to such great lengths for a sip, Thrasher says that she does not like alcohol. "I don't know why I drink. I get sick, but I still drink.

"A lot of my friends are gone through drinking. They were drowned or froze or were hit by a car."

Thrasher now drinks with her husband, Ronald Asselin, and his cousin, whom Thrasher calls "cous-in-law." She calls her husband "Daddy," because "I love him," and he calls her "Mom."

The timid and small Ronald and the loud and solid 220-pound Margaret do not remember exactly when they were married, but it was sometime in the 1970s. "I thought he was a white man at first,"

Thrasher said of her Metis husband. "But I knew he was a good man because he was quiet."

"She is tough and I always liked a tough woman," Asselin said of his wife, who is part Inuit.

The couple live as squatters in a small one-room shack on public land, on the shores of Great Slave Lake. Behind their home is a trendy city neighbourhood, where the average house lists for $250,000. City Hall tried to evict them until Thrasher barged into the mayor's office, banged her fist on his desk and told him to leave her house alone. "I told him that I had my rights because I was in Yellowknife first," she said. She broke down and cried in front of the mayor, who did not argue. Since then, Thrasher's estate has not been disturbed.

Inside, her home is kept tidy. It has a woodstove, double bed, sofa chair and furnishings from the city dump, including a wall hanging of the Last Supper. Thrasher visits the dump once a week to look for home improvements. She used to eat food from the dump as well, but her face broke out and people called her "Pimple Face." Her features have been further scared by severe frost bite and once a can of spray paint blew up in her face. "The metal got stuck in my lips and my glasses went flying off and I was lifted right off the ground; and you know how heavy I am. It was just like a Bazooka."

Other injuries include a knife wound to the torso, which was inflicted while she was helping a girl who was being attacked by a man, and various bumps and bruises from fending off drunks who have tried to steal her wine. One time she broke her hand by punching a wall after missing a would-be wine thief. Since 1987, she has walked with a limp because of a lame leg and knee that has been repeatedly kicked.

Thrasher can have a violent temper when she has been drinking and is in a bad mood. In 1988, she was convicted of assault causing bodily harm after she cut a woman's lip by throwing a chair at her head. During one of her two earlier common assaults, Thrasher threatened to shoot a man with a .22 calibre rifle. She has also been convicted of four thefts, a break and enter and two possessions of stolen property. She and her husband read the Lost and Found section of the newspaper classifieds to see if they could get something for free that they may have "lost" or if they could get a reward for something they may have "found."

Three charges of causing a disturbance in a public place and five charges under the Northwest Territories Liquor Ordinance round out her record, and she has received further sentences for failing to appear in court and failing to comply with probation orders.

She has been fined anywhere from $10 to $500, but since she is usually broke, she often asks the judge to extend the payment period. Once, after telling the judge that "I just found a job and I'm getting paid $25 every Friday," she was given four extra months to pay a $100 fine for shouting and disrupting the peace of a local cafeteria. But when the four months passed she needed even more time. "I don't want to go back to jail," she told the judge. "Please help, please. I'm trying really hard to work."

Thrasher tries to run away from the police when they spot her drinking in public. Once, with a Mountie in hot pursuit, she ran into a lake. "I just about drowned," she said. "I went down twice. It's a good thing the constable was there. He pulled me out by the hair. He saved my life.

"The RCMP are all very good. They watch us when we're drunk and take us to the drunk tank when we're freezing.

"The doctor tells me that I'm lucky to be alive, and the judge, too."

Doctors in Yellowknife "knocked me out" and gave Thrasher a hysterectomy after she had had "about ten" children. All her babies were put up for adoption and she does not know any of their whereabouts. "That old husband of mine says it's my own fault. He says, 'I told you you shouldn't have gone to the hospital.'

"I still want kids," she said in 1988, at the age of forty. "But I guess it's better this way because my place isn't big enough for kids and sometimes there's no wood (for heat)."

Thrasher herself weighed ten pounds and fifteen ounces when she was born in 1947. She is the youngest in a very large family. "I can't count my brothers and sisters. I think there's twenty-two of us. Maybe there's only fifteen, who knows." Her parents were heavy drinkers who took along their children to taverns so they would not have to drink alone. Thrasher's mother, an Inuk from Alaska, and her father, a Portuguese fisherman and whaler, raised their family in the communities of Aklavik and Inuvik on the Mackenzie River delta. Thrasher went to Catholic mission schools there and learned to sketch and paint. She still draws and sells her artwork on the streets of Yellowknife.

Thrasher dropped out of school and left Inuvik when she was a teenager to take care of her mother, who was sent to a hospital in Edmonton with high blood pressure and, later, blindness. Most of the

1960s were wasted away in Edmonton, where she started drinking while living with a man who beat her. She eventually left him and returned north sometime in the early 1970s — she does not remember exactly when. (The first entry into her Yellowknife criminal record was May 5, 1973.) By the late 1970s, Thrasher had become the best known personality in the city. When she is not drinking, she can usually be found chatting with passers-by in front of the post office or the public library. "The tourists are the best. I shake hands with them, smile at them, and they take my picture."

At the Gold Range — the rowdiest, toughest tavern in town and the only one that has not permanently banned Thrasher — she is cheered on by beer-drinking patrons as she belts out blues songs such as "Big Mama" at a jam session held every Saturday afternoon.

While a popular novelty act on the stage and in the streets, Thrasher, and her husband, and the lifestyle they lead, are also the butt of many jokes in Yellowknife. "I know people put us down, but we've never been on welfare or unemployment. I don't believe in it. I'd rather shovel snow or sweep sidewalks," she said.

Local store owners often pay Thrasher and her husband to clear their doorways. And in the summer, City Hall pays them each $24 a day, through a contract with the Salvation Army, to sweep sidewalks and street gutters. In 1988, the city planned to cancel the contract, which "hurt my feelings deep in my heart," Thrasher said. "It's the best job I've had in my life. No matter what, I'm going to get it back."

Over 200 people signed a petition and she was soon back sweeping the streets. Since the quality of her work was never questioned, Thrasher supposed that City Hall was out to hassle her because she had run for mayor in the previous municipal election. Her platform was to provide homes for the homeless. "We need to build something for them where they can eat and sleep and not get kicked out," she said.

She promised she would stop drinking if elected, but when asked on the campaign trail what she would do about the problem of loiterers at the library, she said: "Send them to the Legion."

The election bid did not cost her a cent — in fact she made a profit. She sold her campaign buttons and posters, initially for one dollar each but demand soon pushed the price up to five dollars. One person paid $30 for a poster of a close-up shot of Thrasher wearing one of her six headbands. She started wearing the headbands that year "so I don't get headaches."

Thrasher collected 248 votes — fourth out of five candidates, but not far behind the second and third place finishers. The newly elected mayor considered Thrasher's surprising support to be a protest vote. "I think it was sort of a Rhinoceros vote if anything," she said.

Thrasher takes herself somewhat more seriously than her opponents. After the controversy over the street cleaning contract, she said that she would run for mayor again. "And this time I'll win."

SHARON FIRTH: FROM A TRAPLINE TO THE OLYMPICS

Sharon Firth's Order of Canada insignia is tucked away inside a bag in a storage room, along with her thirty-seven national cross-country ski medals.

"Sure, I appreciate them, but there's really nothing I can do with them," said the four-time Olympian, who, along with her identical twin sister, Shirley, dominated Nordic skiing in Canada for nearly two decades.

After retiring in 1985, Firth was more concerned with re-adjusting to the long, cold winters and the slow pace of life back in the North, than basking in past glories. It would be a difficult transition, not unlike the one she made twenty years earlier. Then she was a young Loucheaux girl who had been raised on a trapline on the Mackenzie River delta in a family of twelve children. Never having even heard of the Olympic games, she suddenly found herself enduring the hectic pace of the international ski circuit.

Firth is a product of a government-funded experiment that was set up to "motivate young native people to higher achievements through competitive athletics." Cross-country skiing was the chosen programme because the northern land and climate made for ideal ski conditions. And besides, the students seemed to enjoy it. So said ski coach Bjorger Pettersen shortly after leaving a corporate executive job in Norway to come to Inuvik, N.W.T., in 1967 to run the Territorial Experimental Ski Training, or TEST, programme: "The northern people have always been nomadic. They have for centuries been travelling long distances over the snow. Among their past's most heroic feats are the long runs after caribou and behind dog teams. This past environment has adapted the northern people with a special ability to relax between their movements — one of the most important aspects of cross-country skiing techniques."

Sharon Firth signed up for the TEST programme after school one day because "all my friends were doing it," she recalled.

"I had never heard of skiing before. At that time I had no idea what was going on. I just showed up for the training because it was something different and it was fun."

The TEST programme turned into the Inuvik Ski Club, which evolved into the Northwest Territories Ski Team. In the late 1960s, northern skiers dominated Canadian junior championships, and the Firth sisters beat top American skiers in North American competitions. They competed through the experimental programme until 1969, when a national women's cross-country ski team was formed. The sixteen-year-old Firth sisters were the team's first members and Pettersen was its first coach. "They really only had us to choose from," Sharon said.

The Nordic ski team did not have much money in its early days. TEST's annual budget was $52,000. (It took $2 million to produce Nancy Greene, the Canadian alpine ski star of the 1960s.) "We really didn't have any support group," Sharon said. "When the men were racing, we were out there helping them with timing, and feeding them at the longer races. And when we raced, the men were always out there helping us."

Her first overseas trip was to Scandinavia. She did not know what to expect. "People were so kind to us all the time. Never in their lives did they see Indians or Eskimos. I think some of them thought we were still from the wild, wild west. And because Shirley and I were twin sisters, we were quite popular."

While other northern native skiers who came up through the TEST programme suffered culture shock, the Firth sisters thrived in the new world they encountered through skiing. "I remember that I wanted my life to be better than what I saw in the North," Sharon said. "I certainly didn't want to be a trapper and live off the land. That's a hard life."

By 1970 it was clear to coach Pettersen that the TEST programme was a success: "Their efforts, dedication and hard work have set and are setting an extraordinary example for other northern youth to follow; and with Olympic gold on the horizon they are surely proving that their races have gone far beyond the illusion of the smiling Eskimo and the drifting Indian."

The Firths never did bring home the Olympic medal that their coach predicted. At their first Olympics, the 1972 winter games in Sapporo, Japan, nineteen-year-old Sharon still was not sure what the Olympics were all about. "To me, it was just another race with some big name." And the Indian twins on skis were still an international novelty. They spent much of their time giving media interviews.

During the next three winter Olympics — at Innsbruk in 1976, Lake Placid in 1980, and Sarajevo in 1984 — a more experienced Sharon Firth realized that the games were rare opportunities to test herself against the world's best. She trained hard, but still, neither she nor her sister could handle the pressure of the Olympics. "We were the best in Canada and everyone expected so much from us. You would get all these telegrams and you start thinking, 'Am I doing it for them or am I doing it for me?' All these sorts of things go through your head and it's a distraction."

Sharon's best Olympic finish was a twenty-first place in the twenty-kilometre race in 1984. She usually finished in the top fifteen, and often the top ten, in international competitions.

The 1980 games were her most disappointing. The Canadian Olympic Association did not send a men's Nordic ski team to Lake Placid. It did not decide to send four women, including the Firths, until two weeks before the Olympics were to begin. "The coaches they had there during the Olympics didn't like the girls on the team. They told us that if we didn't do well, we would all be kicked off the team. We had to put up with that for two weeks. It was like banging your head against the wall."

Pettersen retired as coach in 1975, and Firth did not get along with the new coaches. "They treated us like babies. They wanted us to wake up at a certain time, go running at a certain time, go to bed at a certain time. We definitely had the motivation for training, we didn't have to be pushed. By then it had come naturally."

The coaches wanted to replace Sharon and Shirley with younger skiers. "They said we weren't good enough anymore. They figured we were in it too long and we were too old. But nobody ever beat us. There still isn't anyone who has done better than us. Maybe there was some prejudice there."

The Firths were seen as country hicks by national team officials who were now producing their own skiers from southern Canadian centres. "We tried to not let it get to us. We just thought, 'fine, if that's the way you're going to think, then we'll prove that we're better people,'" Sharon said. "When you get right down to it, there was just Shirley and I who helped each other."

The pressure was too much for Sharon Firth in 1978. She quit the team. But she was "pretty lonely" without her sister, who was sending her postcards from around the world, and she started training again. She made the team the following year, "which was a real struggle because they sure didn't want me back."

After the disastrous 1980 Olympics, the Firths found renewed hope. Dome Petroleum was active in the Beaufort Sea at the time and was conscious of its corporate image in and around Inuvik. The oil company, along with the government of the Northwest Territories, became the Firths' financial sponsors. It meant they were no longer at the mercy of the national team. "We had the freedom to go to the races and training camps by ourselves without all these nagging people bothering us," Sharon said. "I did better when the national team wasn't involved, because they didn't support us anyway."

Her best season was in 1982 when "I just had it altogether." When sister Shirley retired in 1984, Sharon decided to ski the marathon circuit for one more season. She coached herself and won the overall national title. "It just proves you can do it without all those officials wanting to be a part of you, and saying, 'oh, that was my athlete. I coached her.'"

Behind her dazzling smile, Sharon Firth is not unfriendly, but difficult to get to know. She was a loner on the ski circuit, reluctant to socialize or trade training tips with either her team-mates or foreign competitors. "They couldn't understand why people lived up north and I was never really interested in talking about skiing all the time," she said. "You can think skiing and talk skiing all day. Everything is skiing, skiing, skiing. There's more to life than skiing... When you stop competitive racing, you have to start dealing with the real world."

Retired from the ski circuit at age thirty-one, Sharon Firth went knocking on doors for a job. She had been on the national ski team for seventeen years and had won thirty-seven medals. She had received the Order of Canada and there was even a portrait of her and her sister hanging in the Inuvik town hall. But when she went to look for a job, all she heard was that she only had a high school education.

She was employed briefly to recruit native people to work at the Northwest Territories pavilion at Expo '86 in Vancouver. After the world's fair, her striking appearance led to some modelling jobs, but they were not permanent either. Then she worked as a store cashier. She eventually signed up for an on-the-job training position in Yellowknife with the Workers' Compensation Board, at which, she said, "I'll survive."

Yet Sharon takes a positive approach to her post-skiing life. "I've spent half my life trying to be good at one thing and now there are so many other things that I want to try and that I'd like to be good at."

Sister Shirley married a Swedish representative of a multinational ski manufacturing company and moved to the French Riviera, where she is raising a family. It was the first time the twin sisters were permanently separated. "We miss each other, we write and phone each other a lot, but you can't just sit and vegetate," Sharon said. "We lead our own lives now. We may even be closer now, emotionally."

The twins shared an apartment in Banff, Alberta, when they were not living out of a suitcase during their skiing days. There was the occasional case of sibling rivalry, but not on the ski course. "Once you're in a race, you compete against yourself. Once you start competing against another person, I think you fail. You have to do it for yourself."

Firth's do-it-yourself approach to skiing, training, and life are rooted in the early TEST programme. The experiment worked, so why, she wondered, did it drop from sight? Nothing like it exists today. Winter games between competitors from the Northwest Territories, Yukon and Alaska are held every two years, but they are as much drunken parties as athletic events. Firth returned north and saw young people overwhelmed with social problems that she could not have imagined when she was growing up — alcohol abuse, glue sniffing, school drop-outs, suicide. "Nowadays, kids are not motivated. The mentality today isn't to be achievers."

It is unlikely that other Olympians will come out of the North in the near future. That might be just as well, Sharon thought, should they be put through the same frustrations she had to face. Firth watched the Calgary Olympics in February 1988 from the stands. "I was really happy to be on the outside looking in. It's such a high level of competition. Athletes are pushed so hard and when you're all finished, there's no glory."

Sharon Firth skis strictly for pleasure now, once a week in the winter, if that.

"It depends on the temperature."

BEZAL JESUDASON: HOW TO GET TO THE NORTH POLE

Anyone planning a trip to the North Pole should talk to a man who grew up near the equator.

Bezal Jesudason earns his living by helping people reach the top of the world. He sends supplies to his northbound clients and keeps track of their progress by satellite surveillance and radio transmission.

It does not matter how they travel. A Japanese man wanted to be the first person to ride a motorcycle to the North Pole. He went to Jesudason, who told him he could do it if he had two Inuit guides following him on snowmobiles to carry his fuel. In the spring of 1987, Shinji Kazama rode his $100,000 custom-made motorcycle to the North Pole in twenty-four days.

Earlier, a British walking expedition did not seek Jesudason's advice. The trip was called off after several days because of severe frostbite to the feet of one of its members. "None of the people I've ever helped got frostbitten feet," assured Jesudason. "I come from a warm climate, but I know how to keep myself from freezing."

Jesudason was born and raised in Madras, a city of several million people in southern India. He immigrated to Canada and headed north in 1968, when he was twenty-seven years old, to take a maintenance job with the government. After a decade as a northern civil servant, he became a tourist operator of sorts at Resolute Bay, a government weather station and a community of about one hundred Inuit in the high Arctic. He and his wife Terry planned to run a small hotel and offer tourists a five-day snowmobile trip from Resolute to Grise Fiord, the only other community above the Northwest Passage. They still do that, but in 1978, during their first year of operation, they also were asked to outfit Naomi Uemeura of Japan. He took a team of dogs to the North Pole and became the first person to have done the journey alone.

Uemeura also was the first person to have undisputed proof that he conquered the Pole because he was the first to be tracked by satellite. (In 1909, Robert Peary and Frederick Cook both claimed to reach the Pole first. It will never be known who won the race, or if either of them made it at all.) Now, everyone who travels to the Pole carries a 700-gram satellite transmitter, supplied by Jesudason. Through a computer linked to Washington D.C., which in turn is linked to the satellite hook-up, Jesudason receives the traveller's precise location and coded messages detailing such matters as weather and ice conditions and food and equipment supply.

Most visitors to the North Pole leave from an ice-covered rock 800 kilometers away known as Ward Hunt Island, at the northern-most tip of North America. They must complete their trip between the first week of March, when the sun reappears from its winter sleep, and late May, when the Arctic ice pack begins to break.

Since 1982, mad races to the North Pole have become an annual event with an unusual cast of characters. Along with Kazama the motorcyclist, those who have made it include various dog teams and walking and skiing expeditions from Finland, Norway and the United States, two flying Frenchmen in ultra-light aircraft and an Australian millionaire in a helicopter.

A five-foot, two-inch Japanese movie actress spent two months camping out in a tent near Resolute Bay to prepare for a snowmobile trip to the Pole in 1985. Enroute she battled fog, whiteouts, temperature extremes between -14 C and -70 C, and ice ridges and ice obstacles twice her size over which she had to haul her snowmobile and equipment. She came within 100 kilometers of her goal, but had to abandon it after running into broken ice and open water.

"I know technology has made it much safer to travel in the Arctic, but mother nature is still much stronger," said Jesudason, who is full of worry and concern whenever an expedition is on its way. His "scattered brain" helps him cope with both his worries and the non-stop pace of his work — dealing with broken snowmobiles, talking to expeditions over the radio, talking to future expeditions over the telephone, setting up expeditions' base camps, hiring Inuit guides and so on. "I have to be doing ten different things at once, like a seal that has ten different holes in the ice to come up and breathe from," he said.

Jesudason believes that anything is possible if it is well planned, well financed, and if the weather cooperates. One German trekker slept every night for a month in a walk-in freezer set at -51 degrees Celsius to prepare for his Arctic venture. Although the conditions were not comparable, Jesudason thought that he had the right attitude.

"But money is the most important thing of all. Most people fail because of a lack of money," he said. People should not even consider travelling across the ice to the North Pole unless they have at least $150,000 in the bank. "Don't misunderstand me, they're not giving it to Bezal. Any little thing can happen, like they accidentally leave the radio on and drain the batteries. It would cost $20,000 to fly them $20 worth of batteries."

"Everyone asks me, 'Bezal, what's next?' I tell them that I'm going to go by elephant. This is the joke that's been going around the Arctic the past couple of years. But if somebody defies me, I'll prove that they are wrong. I can do it with elephants. It'll just take more money and more planning."

The cheapest and easiest way to get to the North Pole is to fly directly there in a twin-engine aircraft. Wealthy arm-chair adventurers, mostly American corporate executives, spend $10,000 each for a bumpy twenty-hour flight from Resolute — ten hours of looking out a window at the mountainous Ellesmere Island and then another ten of nothing but ice. They stand at the North Pole for thirty minutes and drink champagne, and then get back into the plane for the twenty-hour ride back.

Air and land travellers alike go to the North Pole to fulfill some sort of dream. They are the type of people who "would walk to the moon if they could," Jesudason said. The North Pole captures the imagination because it really is the top of the world. Every way you look is south. No country or person owns the North Pole — it is in the middle of the Arctic Ocean. All the world's time zones converge there, so it is every time of the day all at the same moment.

People derive more pleasure from going there if they can claim to be a "first." A Louisiana man confined to a wheelchair and his seven-year-old son once flew to the North Pole. He was the first handicapped person there, and his son was the youngest.

Fewer than 400 people have ever been to the Pole. Jesudason has visited four times, each by plane. On such trips, however, he must contend with "Archie Bunker-types" who ask the inevitable stupid question. They ask if they will see a pole sticking out of the ground. Or they do not realize that the Pole is in an ocean and wonder if they have to climb a hill to get to it. "North Americans are bad at geography," he said. "If someone is going to spend $10,000, you would expect they would learn something about the place before they came."

He has told travellers to the Magnetic North Pole that they will know when they have reached their destination because their pants will fall down if they keep keys and coins in their pockets.

Since the mid-1980s, people with unorthodox opinions of mental and physical health started travelling to the Magnetic Pole, about 1300 kilometers below the true North Pole but "only" 700 kilometers northwest of Resolute. A university professor from Hong Kong was conducting experiments to see if an ancient Chinese exercise called Qi-qong had any scientific validity. The theory is based on the idea that the human body has a magnetic pole, similar to the earth's magnetic pole. From this it follows that a bodyache will go away if someone touches you because that person's hand gives off magnetic waves. Theoretically, the effect would be intensified at the Magnetic North Pole, and so in 1987 the professor went there for a few weeks with an assortment of electronic equipment and gadgets. Jesudason mentioned to him that the Magnetic North Pole moved about fifty kilometers a day in a clock-wise motion. The professor thought this might explain why the needle point in acupuncture changed every twenty-four hours, and he returned the following year to conduct further experiments.

Several years earlier, a woman from Montreal who believed in a new science called geo-biology asked Jesudason to suit her up for a trip to the Magnetic North Pole while all the planets were lined up in a certain position. "She actually told me she was going to the Magnetic North Pole for a fast tune-up. It sounded like Speedy Muffler King, the way she was talking," Jesudason said.

"It's very easy to say they're all eccentrics or nuts. I sometimes think it, but I don't know if it's right to say it. They can believe it if they want to. When Galileo said the world was round, it was the same thing, people laughed at him."

Following the scientists and the cults to the Magnetic North Pole have been the adventure seekers and fly-in tourists. It is closer and more accessible than the real thing, "but nobody really cares about the Magnetic North Pole," Jesudason said. "Everyone knows the compass points to the north, but if you took the three billion people in the world,

I'd bet less than ten thousand would know there was a Magnetic North Pole."

Most travellers to either the magnetic or the geographic pole come from the well-to-do nations of the world. "I can tell the world economy just by sitting up here. When the German economy was the best, there were a lot of Germans here. Now it's the Japanese. Most of our customers were American, but there hasn't been as many since the stock market crash in 1987."

Jesudason observes almost with humour the different cultural and national characteristics. It may be true that the Americans are obnoxious, but the British, like the one with frostbitten feet, are the worst. "If you look at history, the Norwegians always learned from the Greenlanders. They learned to use dogs from the Eskimos, who were using them for hundreds and thousands of years. And then you find Roald Amundsen travelling through the North with dogs and you find Robert Scott taking his horses and ponies (on the ill-fated expedition to the South Pole in 1910). And you see pictures of Sir John Franklin and he's always wearing his brass buttons and carrying silver cutlery. It's absolutely impractical. That sort of thing goes right down to the modern-day British people. They won't learn any of the ways of the local people. If I'm going to climb Mount Everest, I can't do it without the Sherpas. The Sherpas are the ones who have lived there for years."

The Inuit are the Sherpas of the Arctic. Time-tested Inuit technology is needed to make it to the North Pole by dog team or snowmobile. To pull his luggage, the traveller needs a komatik — a sled that used to be made of whale bone with ivory runners, but is now built from lumber with plastic runners. However, the principle has not changed. The sled is tied loosely together with ropes so it can turn, bend and bump over ridges of ice.

Jesudason often hires local Inuit hunters as guides. The Inuit do it for boasting rights in the community, and for the money. A guide can earn $10,000 for taking somebody to the North Pole. The Japanese actress also threw in her snowmobile as a tip.

An Inuit guide also is accustomed to a $1,000 tip for taking a Saudi Arabian sheik or American big game hunter on a polar bear hunt. The easy money only encourages poor work ethics, according to Jesudason. He thinks that it is government's fault. When he first came north, Jesudason worked as a maintenance man for an entire community. He repaired anything that was broken in public housing, in the school, or at the airport. During the 1970s, the government set up new departments and each one had to maintain its own buildings. One job was split into several. "Someone now probably makes 30,000 bucks to maintain the runway at the Toronto airport and someone else probably gets the same to clear snow at the Grise Fiord airstrip. The job description is the same — they've got to maintain the airport. But the amount of traffic that goes into Grise Fiord is one plane a week, if that."

Jesudason has a special government rate at his hotel — $105 a night. Tourists paying out of their own pockets are charged $75. And when his taxes or utility fees are raised, he increases the government rate. "I take my vengeance out on them that way. I tell them that if I have to follow their regulations, then this is what it's going to cost them.

"I'm just a one-man fight against the goddamn government."

Among autographed photographs of the various North Pole expeditions, Jesudason has a fifteen-year-old comic strip pinned to his office wall that depicts an Inuk building, an igloo, in the middle of the tundra. A man in a suit and tie carrying a briefcase flies by in a helicopter and asks, "Do you have a building permit?"

"It was a joke then, but it has almost come to pass," Jesudason said.

By the late 1980s, the Northwest Territories government had launched an aggressive world-wide marketing campaign to promote tourism to the North. But, Jesudason said, neither the small communities nor the fragile environment can cope with large groups of camera-toting tourists. The marketing strategy, he predicted, will destroy the North's greatest attraction: its mystique.

In 1986, Parks Canada created a national park reserve at the north end of Ellesmere Island. That will attract many people who will come and trample across one of the most fragile ecosystems in the world, Jesudason said. "Fine, call it a park and leave it alone. But now they're advertising it and building shacks for the park wardens.

"It's a good thing Mount Everest is in a poor country like Nepal and not in Canada, or else there would be a Hilton hotel on top."

Jesudason claimed that he would leave the North without hesitation if his life became too frustrating. "I came with nothing, I'll go back with nothing — that's what the Bible says. I'll bulldoze all my things into the ocean. I won't give them to anybody."

Jesudason said that he has seen the North in better times, but, he admitted, "it's still very nice compared to anywhere further south."

And really, he cannot go any farther north.